Religious and Moral Education

THE LIBRARY OF EDUCATION

A Project of The Center for Applied Research in Education, Inc.

Categories of Coverage

I	II	III
Curriculum and Teaching	Administration, Organization, and Finance	Psychology for Educators

IV	V	VI
History, Philosophy, and Social Foundations	Professional Skills	Educational Institutions

Religious and Moral Education

MARVIN J. TAYLOR

Saint Paul School of Theology Methodist
Kansas City, Missouri

The Center for Applied Research in Education, Inc.
New York

LIBRARY OF CONGRESS
CATALOG CARD NO.: 65-25729

PRINTED IN THE UNITED STATES OF AMERICA

Foreword

From the beginning of our history the place of moral and spiritual values in education has been a matter of central concern to the American people. Conceptions of the relationship of religion to these values have changed with the increasing complexity of our common life, the diversification of religious beliefs and practices, and the acceptance of responsibility for universal education by the total community.

In Colonial times the term "religious education"—as distinguished from "secular"—would have had little meaning, since practically all formal education was sponsored by the churches and religious ideas and symbols pervaded the entire school curriculum. So long as homogeneity of religion was typical, the affinity of religion and education could cause little difficulty. But diversity of religion, rather than homogeneity, has become characteristic of the modern community. Today most Americans tend to make a distinction between religious and secular education and to allocate responsibility for the former to the churches and for the latter to the state. But separation of the functions of church and state in education has proved to be a most perplexing problem.

Attempts to solve this problem have resulted in a wide variety of administrative arrangements and curricular patterns. Different groups have endeavored to preserve their religious heritage in various ways, ranging all the way from support of public schools, with only a minimum of supplementary religious teachings, to complete separation and the maintenance of a parallel system of parochial schools. Public school leaders have attempted to provide for moral and spiritual values within an increasingly pluralistic culture in ways that range from integration of religious subject matter into the public school curriculum to a complete disavowal of responsibility for religious teaching. Some religious groups have insisted that religion be given much greater emphasis in the curriculum; others contend that specific reference to religion is a violation of the principle of separation of church and state. Some types of accommodation have become the bases for litigation, and the courts have wrestled with problems of definition and interpretation. Apparent contradictions and ambiguities in court decisions have created wide confusion over some of the basic issues.

Publications dealing with religious and moral education are voluminous; writers often view the issues through the colored glasses of their own prejudices; and the casual reader needs a reliable guide through the maze of conflicting opinions in order to reach valid conclusions of his own.

In the present volume, Dr. Taylor has successfully condensed and combined the most relevant materials, has placed the issues in historical perspective, and has outlined the most promising of the current options. His book will undoubtedly prove to be a permanently valuable contribution to the literature of American education.

LAWRENCE C. LITTLE

Chairman, Program in
Religious Education
University of Pittsburgh

Religious and Moral Education

Marvin J. Taylor

In the field of education an unusual paradox has arisen. Although moral issues in the country today are becoming more prominent the public schools are becoming more secular!

Evidence of increasing moral sensitivity is accumulating. Legislatures are asked to lay down codes of ethics to guide men in office who are frequently confronted with conflicts in public and private interest. Students, especially at the college and university level, have become involved in public issues as never before in our history, from race issues in Alabama and Mississippi to international policy in Viet Nam. Their participation in peace marches, ban-the-bomb demonstrations, and sit-ins—and now the "teach-in"—shows a sensitivity to moral issues as never before.

And yet coincident with this growth the public schools reached a new point of secularization when prayers were recently banned from the school routine by the United States Supreme Court. In an increasingly secularized world there is a tendency to regard religious and moral instruction as a supplementary rather than a principal service of the schools. Historically this was not always the case. In the greater part of the Christian era, education found its chief end that of religious and moral instruction. If it has lost that eminence in America it is to schismatic and sectarian influences within the community of religiously-minded people rather than to hostility of the political state that one must lay the blame.

Differences of opinion in religious and moral instruction usually stem from metaphysical and theological views which are so sharp that partisans or sectarians trust only themselves to state the bases on which their respective faiths rest. On this account the authorship of a volume like the present one is a very delicate matter. Professor Marvin J. Taylor has handled this difficult assignment with unusual candor and balance. To make doubly sure that he has stated views other than his own accurately and appealingly he has submitted various chapters devoted specifically to different points of view for review and approval by men who share them. We may hope that his efforts will add to a growing ecumenism and thus to the elimination of the paradox with which we started.

JOHN S. BRUBACHER
Content Editor

Contents

CHAPTER I

The History of American
Religious Education

Religion and education have been inevitable partners wherever
men have lived, for when religion is defined as that to which one
gives his ultimate devotion and loyalty, then it is only natural that
he will want to perpetuate it. Education has been the medium that
man has used to initiate the young into the ceremonies, beliefs, customs, and all other facets of religious observance.

Not only has this partnership of religion and education been
noted in other cultures and traditions, but it is also evident in America's Judeo-Christian heritage. The writer of Proverbs reflected an
ancient concern for education when he penned: "Keep hold of instruction, do not let her go; guard her, for she is your life" (4:13).
This thought was repeated by the author of Deuteronomy who
summed up the family's long established educational responsibilities
with "you shall teach them diligently to your children, and shall talk
of them when you sit in your house, and when you walk by the
way, and when you lie down, and when you rise" (6:7). It was this
strong concern for preserving the faith that the early Christian
church inherited.

Christian history has revealed an often bewildering variety of
ways by which this duty might be performed. At times the role of
the parents has been dominant; on other occasions schools were established by the Church. But always there has been an interest in
the instruction of the young. Since the beginning of the Christian
era this emphasis has been strong in both Jewish and Christian cultures. It was this influence that the original colonists brought with
them to the New World in the sixteenth and seventeenth centuries.

The Colonial Period

The religious and educational patterns which were established in
the colonies are usually divided into three types by historians. Each
reflects not only its European origins but also the cultural and reli-

1

gious composition of its settlers. Thus, New England, the Middle
Atlantic, and the South each used a different type of organization.

Calvinistic theology dominated the New England mind, and the
Massachusetts Bay Colony, for example, borrowed the Genevan
theocratic ideas in which there was a close alliance between the
state and the one established church. The government gave a portion of collected taxes to support the church, and the state's power
was used to enforce both the prevailing doctrines and religious practices. When, in 1642, the need for religious nurture was felt, it was
the colonial legislature which required that children acquire the
"ability to read and understand the principles of religion." This act
was followed in 1647 by the quaintly worded Old Deluder Act
which ordered schools for the express purpose of thwarting Satan
who was described as that "old deluder of men's minds."

This affinity of religion for education is further demonstrated by
the educational materials used. The original text was the Hornbook
containing the alphabet, numerals, and the Lord's Prayer. The most
commonly used primer was *The New England Primer,* best known
for its rhymed approach to the alphabet, starting with: "In Adam's
fall, we sinned all." It has been described as being 99 per cent religious, and this was supplemented with *The Shorter Catechism* and
John Cotton's famous theological treatise, *Spiritual Milk for American Babes Drawn Out of the Breasts of Both Testaments for Their
Souls' Nourishment.* All were widely used in these "public" schools.

But the religious homogeneity of settlers did not prevail in the
middle colonies. The Quaker colony, Pennsylvania, clearly illustrates this difference. English, Dutch, Swedes, Germans and others
came, each bringing with them their religious variations. Quakers,
Presbyterians, Moravians, Mennonites, Lutherans, Baptists, Catholics and other denominations settled there. Since in their homelands
the church and the school were closely connected, this pattern prevailed. These were in effect parish or parochial schools, sponsored
by local congregations rather than towns or other governmental
agencies. Both interest in and quality of education tended to vary
from group to group and town to town, but the motivation was almost always religious in nature. The Bible, the catechism, and other
theological documents were the texts used, and the goals centered
on Christian literacy and the perpetuation of the faith and the
Church. Except for some very early efforts at state establishment
of schools in both New York and Pennsylvania, public control
tended throughout the Colonial period to be nominal and limited.

Schools were the province of the churches, except for the licensing of teachers and other similar administrative controls.

The South reveals still a third major type of educational control. Virginia may be cited as the example. Its colonists were not as religiously motivated as the northern settlers. They brought the established Church of England with them, and therefore a close alliance of government and church. The schools which appeared were under Anglican control, much as those in their homeland. Teachers were licensed by the clerical authorities to guarantee their theological acceptibility. The wealthy plantation owners and great landholders secured private tutors for their children. And the only "public" schools which existed were for the families of the very poor, the charity schools maintained by the church. Compared with New England, this was a rather rigidly structured class society in which the more democratic "common" school had no place. The state itself played little part in their development, support or control.[1]

Although it is accurate to make this three-fold division among the colonies, it must not be concluded that the separations are mutually exclusive. Almost all of these schools were church schools in a most important way. It was the sense of religious urgency which produced them, and the study of religion played a preponderant role in their course of study. And even in New England where government was the controlling body, there was a virtual establishment of Puritan religion. The government spoke for the church, and the church's goals were those implemented by civil action. Hence, the Colonial period may well be summarized as a time when education depended largely on organized religion for its impetus, its spirit, its funds, and its reason for being. The inevitable partnership of religion and education was here demonstrated again.

The Gradual Secularization of Public Education

The process of secularization was both long and complex. The United States shared in the general religious decline of the eighteenth century, and there was a gradually increasing emphasis upon the civic goals of the schools. There was little open rejection of religious content. Rather, the enlargement of the school's objectives left relatively less time and attention for religious instruction. The

---

[1] See R. Freeman Butts, *The American Tradition in Religion and Education* (Boston: Beacon Press, Inc., 1950), pp. 3–67.

effects of the Revolution spurred the process onward. The nation had become a democracy, and an enlightened citizenry was essential. Universal education was clearly the best way to achieve this, and the public education movement resulted. But the schools which existed were by and large religiously oriented. And almost all were sectarian, having been established by or through the influence of the various religious denominations and teaching the tenets of these particular groups.

A major foundational step toward change was taken in the adoption of the First Amendment to the federal Constitution. The separation of church and state was declared, and a system of free, public, tax-supported schools could hardly include religious instruction without violating the spirit of this amendment, in principle at least. But, this idea was implemented only slowly. The struggles in Massachusetts and New York illustrate the dilemma confronting the young nation. By the 1820's the religious homogeneity of the Massachusetts colony had been radically altered, and the children in the public schools represented many denominations. An 1826 legislative enactment directed the continued instruction of children in "piety," but the following year sectarian teaching was banned by law. Since the religious content was distinctly Congregational, a major change was necessary. The duty of enforcing the injunction fell to Horace Mann, the state secretary of education. Although denounced as an atheist, Mann never opposed religious teaching. He said, "I am in favor of religious instruction in our schools to the extremest verge to which it can be carried without invading those rights of conscience which are established by the laws of God and guaranteed to us by the Constitution of the State."[2] Mann held that the Bible was not sectarian, and together with other common elements in Christianity could be included in the public schools. He favored reading the Bible without interpretation, allowing it to speak for itself. Thus, the first stage of secularization was an attempt to eliminate religious particularity while retaining a generally shared Christian consensus in the schools. The effort was soundly criticized from two opposite directions. First, those whose religious tenets had previously prevailed were most reluctant to relinquish their favored position. But others, chiefly (but not exclusively) Roman Catholics, called attention to this basically Protestant approach to biblical centrality and right of private interpretation. The latter group held that

---

[2] Cited by Raymond B. Culver, *Horace Mann and Religion in the Massachusetts Public Schools* (New Haven: Yale University Press, 1929), p. 207.

"nonsectarian" really meant "Protestant" and that all Protestants together actually represented a "sect" or subdivision of Christians. Neither group found the solution to be wholly acceptable.]

In New York City a similar situation existed. There the schools were chiefly private, operated under church auspices and until 1825 with direct financial aid. A Free School Society was established in 1807 to provide education for those children not being reached by the religious institutions. It rapidly became a strong force for free, universal education. And in 1825 the city council withdrew funds from the church schools and channeled all tax funds for education into this Public School Society, as it had become known. Despite its name, the Society was actually a private, philanthropic agency with a strong Protestant bias. Its religious practices included prayer, hymns, and instruction about and reading of the King James Version of the Bible. Even its nonreligious textbooks were filled with derogatory references to Catholics and the Pope. When the situation became intolerable to the Catholics, they felt compelled to withdraw their children from these influences and to establish their own schools. They petitioned the city council for a share of the public funds to support their institutions and were almost unanimously refused. Relief came through a Democrat-Catholic coalition in the state legislature which in 1842 extended to the city the system of state schools administered by a locally elected board. Catholics and some Protestants found a purely secular school, divorced from church control or influence, preferable to the discriminatory practices which confronted them in the Public School Society's institutions.

These two illustrations were not isolated phenomena. The instruction in Christian doctrine, so prevalent during the Colonial period, continued to be important in the thinking of Americans following the Revolution. But there was a gradually emerging recognition that the inclusion of sectarian religious teaching was offensive to the consciences of many citizens. And further, it was in violation of the democratic ideal of freedom of religious exercise, as guaranteed by the First Amendment. As a consequence, by 1860 most of the original colonies had eliminated distinctly doctrinal teachings. Many continued the reading of the Bible, on the premise that this was not sectarian, and continued to provide instruction in morality without specifying any theological sanctions for its validity. In many of the newer states the principle of separation extended somewhat further. Particularly in the West several states have held even Bible reading to be "sectarian" and proscribed in the public schools. As one historian has written, "The educational counterpart of the political divorce of church and state was the exclusion of religion from the public school curriculum."[3] It was a gradual process which extended over much of the nineteenth century throughout the nation, and it posed a genuine problem for the denominations which had learned to rely on these schools during the prerevolutionary decades. The emergence of distinctly church-centered educational institutions was one of the major attempts to solve this problem.

The Development
of Protestant Religious Education

The Sunday School Movement. Although isolated instances of colonial pastors offering instruction to children may be found, the impetus for this movement was imported from England. In Gloucester in 1780 Robert Raikes, a Church of England layman, began his schools for poor children on Sundays. The movement spread to America, and the 1780's witnessed their appearance in various places. The First Day Society was begun in Philadelphia in 1790, and others were rapidly established in the major eastern cities. These were loosely connected, interdenominational organizations for the promotion of Sunday schools. The success of the city Sunday school unions was so great that a national body was formed in 1824, known as the American Sunday School Union. Its goals included the selection of curricula, the publication of suitable materials, and the promotion of Sunday schools throughout the nation— but especially on the rapidly expanding frontier in the Middle West. The Union is remembered particularly for its occasional national conventions, beginning in 1832, where thousands of Sunday school enthusiasts met for inspiration and promotion of the movement. At these sessions a philosophy of Sunday school work gradually began to emerge, stressing the duties of elected officers, administration, best techniques of teaching, and other related considerations. The conventions became international in the 1870's with the attendance of Canadian leaders, and in 1905 the name was changed to The International Sunday School Association.

---

[3] John S. Brubacher, *A History of the Problems of Education* (New York: McGraw-Hill Book Company, 1947), p. 334.

Denominational interest in and support of religious education was slow in appearance. Sunday schools had existed for four decades before the first denominational boards of education were established in the 1820's. These reflected the growing conviction that it was the proper function of churches, rather than volunteer and unofficial groups, to provide religious instruction for their members. This official denominational concern for Sunday school work increased rapidly, and the various cooperating denominations joined hands in 1910 to form the Sunday School Council of Evangelical Denominations. Although the International Association was friendly, it was also totally independent of church control. And in time tension between the two agencies developed. Control was not the sole point of conflict. Their educational policies were also at variance, particularly at the point of identifying an adequate curriculum. The years from 1910 through 1922 were devoted to exploratory efforts at resolving these points of tension. Various complementary and cooperative structures were tried without success, and it was determined finally to merge the two into one organization which would fully represent the interests of both.

Recent Organizational Structures. The merging convention was held in 1922 with more than 7000 delegates in attendance. The new organization took the title of International Sunday School Council of Religious Education, later shorted by the elimination of the words "Sunday School." The functions of both previous agencies were combined, and a single cooperative council now existed for coordinating all religious educational activities, denominational and geographical. Thirty-three denominations were the original constituent members, with a number of others joining after 1922. From this date until 1950 the council performed its functions through a series of departments each of which reflected a specific function of religious education; i.e., the education of children, youth, adults, the development of leadership, and so on. It coordinated state and local council of churches' work through other departments and provided associated sections for the professional meetings of workers in various phases of education. Almost every conceivable facet of Christian education was included.

Throughout the 1930's and 1940's it had become increasingly evident that the denominations needed some central agency which would encompass all Christian life. Education, missions, evangelism, and the like, required coordination which autonomous interdenominational agencies for each could not provide. This unity was accomplished in 1950 by the establishment of the National Council of the Churches of Christ in the United States of America. The International Council of Religious Education was one of several comparable bodies which merged to form the National Council. Today the International Council's former functions are now being performed by the National Council's Division of Christian Education. The division also encompasses the work of the former Missionary Education Movement, the National Protestant Council on Higher Education, the Interseminary Movement, and the various undergraduate Student Christian Movements.

Changing Curriculum Patterns. In the years from 1780 through 1872 the Protestant curriculum situation was diverse and confused. The original materials were the catechisms available in that day. These were replaced briefly by intensive Bible memorization from which the "selected lesson" plan evolved. Sunday school was Bible school in those days, and between 1825 and 1872 the study focused upon a portion of the Bible which had been selected for the day. Selections were usually made for a three-month period on some central theme, and a new topic and passages would then be chosen for the next quarter. Numerous selections were made and published, and there was little coordination among them. One observer has labeled the time as the "Babel period" of Sunday school curriculum.[4]

System was brought to this unorganized condition in 1872 when the Convention adopted the uniform lesson plan. A committee was created to prepare a several-year cycle of lessons which could be used in all age-level classes across the denominations: hence the title "uniform." The committee elected to make Bible content its organizing theme, and it issued a seven-year plan for covering the entire Bible. The committee chose the theme, the scripture to be studied, and a common memory verse. Exposition and publication were left to denominational and independent publishers. This scheme made possible for the first time a systematic, comprehensive, and continuous series of Sunday school lessons on the Bible. Dissatisfaction arose quickly, however. The chief criticism was the neglect of age-levels of pupil growth, interest, and capacity. Steadily mounting opposition was climaxed with the acceptance of a

---

[4] Frank G. Lankard, *A History of the American Sunday School Curriculum* (New York: Abingdon Press, 1927), pp. 175–200.

parallel scheme of graded lessons by the International Sunday School Association in 1908. Now both patterns were available for adoption by individual denominations.

A new review of the curriculum pattern was authorized in 1920. The report of its two-year study recommended that group- or cycle-graded lessons be substituted for the existing closely graded ones, that uniform lessons continue to be issued, and that an entirely new "International Curriculum of Religious Education" be created. This latter project was to include all of the churches' educational programs, not just the Sunday church schools, and be based on the latest developments in educational theory. The new curriculum used as its organizing principle the experience of the learner in his interaction with the world, setting this against previous philosophies which had made a body of subject matter (i.e., the Bible, theological beliefs) the units of learning. The control of experience in changed personal and social living was its goal, rather than the acquisition of knowledge. Research and development proceeded throughout the 1920's in the explication of this theory, and it resulted in the publication of the *International Curriculum Guide* in 1932. This *Guide* was designed to help denominations which desired to study the needs of their members and to construct their own curriculum. Continued study and investigation characterized the 1930's and 1940's producing major alterations of this curriculum theory.[5] (See Chapter V.)

Supplementary Educational Programs. Religious education was almost exclusively Sunday school during the first several decades after 1800. But as the century drew to a close, expansion began. Additional programming for youth started in Portland, Maine, in the Christian Endeavor Society, a nondenominational youth organization. Observing its values, the churches rapidly adopted and adapted the idea in the Oxford League, Epworth League, Baptist Young Peoples Union, and others. Interdenominational cooperation came with the Christian Youth Council of North America in 1926 and the United Christian Youth Movement in 1934.

The freedom of summer vacations from school has always been a challenge to educators, and as early as the 1890's individual churches were holding weekday religious classes during vacation

---

[5] William C. Bower and Percy R. Hayward, *Protestantism Faces Its Educational Task Together* (Appleton, Wisc.: C. C. Nelson Publishing Co., 1949), pp. 1–48, 66–88.

time. The Vacation Church School movement was actually begun in New York City by the church federation's establishment of a committee to promote the summer program.

Weekday religious education also existed sporadically around the country, but the movement originated with the 1914 Gary, Indiana, experiment. Here the public school superintendent, believing religion to be a necessary factor in normal child development, offered to release pupils from the schools on a weekly schedule for instruction by the churches. Individual congregations operated their own schools at first, but soon an interdenominational community board was created to perform this function. The idea spread rapidly across the nation with classes being held in both local church and school buildings.

The expansion of religious education also included other uses of the summer months. The International Sunday School Association opened its Lake Geneva Camp in 1914, and other groups followed quickly. Summer conferences for youth and adults were also held, often at camps but also on denominational college campuses. In brief, the 40 years beginning with 1880 saw the religious education movement expand its original Sunday school idea far beyond this relatively narrow program.

The Development of
Jewish Religious Education

It is virtually impossible to understand the development of American Jewish education without considering the cultural circumstances which produced it. The end of the eighteenth century was a decisive turning point for Jews. Up to this time they had resided in all-Jewish ghettos and were isolated from the surrounding culture. Their educational patterns were almost exclusively religious, being confined to a mastery of sacred literature which had piety as its object. But with their emancipation (1791 in France, with other European nations following in succeeding decades) came freedom and citizenship. Inevitably attitudes toward education changed to match these new conditions.

Immigration to America was slow. Relatively few Jews entered during the Colonial period, although a synagogue was built in New York in 1728. Although the nineteenth century did not witness a steady increase, since there was considerable fluctuation from decade to decade, the number of Jews in the United States did rise from about two or three thousand in 1800 to more than a million in 1900 and 4 million by the late 1920's.[6] Prompted by various problems, they came from most of the nations of Europe, fleeing deprivation and pogroms and seeking the freedom of which they had heard.

The earliest Jewish settlers found both worship and education to be problems. Synagogues and schools were each needed but economically unfeasible because of the scarcity of supporters. Educated Jews were often urged to emigrate from Europe to become teachers, and where possible non-Jewish private schools were attended. As synagogues were established, schools were frequently dependent upon the rabbis as the teachers of the religious subjects, and non-Jews as instructors of the secular curriculum.

In the United States the Jew found the most complete system of freedom available to him anywhere in the world. His appreciation led him to give his loyalty to the public schools as the proper medium for the education of his children. As one contemporary Jewish educator has suggested, he did this with considerable enthusiasm since he saw the democratic public school as an important door out of the segregated society in which he had lived.[7] The current strong support for the public schools which is offered by the great majority of the Jewish community is doubtless a reflection of this continuing conviction. The only discernible shift away from this support has been the appearance within very recent years of strong interest in the Jewish all-day school. This interest, however, has been expressed by only a small minority of the Jewish community.

The result of turning to public education created two problems. First, the fears of the more traditional had to be allayed. They fully expected the study of secular subjects carried on in a non-Jewish setting to lead to an abandonment of traditional Judaism. Although never completely erased, these fears seldom altered the trend. The second problem was equally serious. An alternative scheme of education had to be created. By the mid-nineteenth century the numbers of Jews, especially in the larger eastern cities, were sufficient to permit this development. Some Jews turned away from the public

---

[6] Claris E. Silcox and Galen M. Fisher, *Catholics, Jews and Protestants* (New York: Harper & Row, Publishers, 1934), pp. 12–22; and Robert M. Frumkin and Joseph S. Roucek, "Contributions from Minorities, Elites, and Special Educational Organizations," in *Heritage of American Education* (ed.) Richard E. Gross (Boston: Allyn and Bacon, Inc., 1962), p. 367.

[7] Eugene B. Borowitz, "Judaic Roots of Modern Education," in Gross, *ibid.,* p. 98.

school and established private Jewish schools which taught both religious and secular subjects, the latter to replace the education lost by failure to attend the public school. Synagogues also borrowed and adapted the Protestant Sunday school pattern with classes offered as a supplement to the weekday public school experience. The congregational afternoon weekday school was introduced as a more intensive religious education program, particularly when children attended one or more afternoons and Sunday morning as well. In the years following the Civil War, public education accelerated the process of secularization. And once this happened, Jewish leaders gave even greater support to the public schools and turned their own programs even farther into supplementary patterns. Finding the United States to be a land of desired freedom, the Jewish community gladly adjusted to the American way of life, one major facet of which was the public school. This process has continued in the twentieth century with the major emphasis being placed on strengthening the varied forms of schools maintained for supplementing the general educational experiences enjoyed by children and youth.[8]

The Development of Roman Catholic Religious Education

The earliest educational efforts by Catholics in America actually antedate the eastern English settlements of the seventeenth century. Florida, Virginia, and New Mexico all received priests and had worship established in the 1500's, with the St. Augustine parish being organized in 1565. Yet Catholics did not find the Colonial period particularly pleasant. Their allegiance to Rome made them suspect, and both political and religious rights were frequently restricted and often denied. Even Maryland, which had been established by Catholics, denied them the right to teach in order "to prevent the growth of Popery." Despite these handicaps, schools were begun early: in Maryland at Saint Mary's in 1640, Newton in 1673, Bohemia Manor in 1744 and New York City in 1684.

Loyalty to the colonists' cause during the Revolution helped to check this attitude, and the First Amendment also brought the beginnings of genuine religious freedom for Catholics. But the early

---

[8] Judah Pilch, "Jewish Religious Education," in *Religious Education: A Comprehensive Survey* (ed.) Marvin J. Taylor (Nashville: Abingdon Press, 1960), pp. 382–383.

national period produced new problems. Catholic immigration had increased rapidly. The estimated 30,000 Catholics of 1787 grew to 195,000 by 1820, 318,000 by 1830, 663,000 by 1840, and 1,606,000 in 1850. And still the numbers swelled, doubling again and again in 1860, 1880, and 1900. Their growth, the fact that many did not speak English and retained a cultural loyalty to a European homeland, and their religion all helped to produce antipathy toward them. The well-meaning Protestants of the American Nativist movement of the mid-1800's sought to "Americanize" the "foreign" Catholics. And this often degenerated into blatant proselytism. The public school was a major means used. It was the democratic institution which prepared all for citizenship, the Common School Movement being in full development. And it included "nonsectarian" (which meant Protestant, in those days) religious instruction, a vital ingredient in the Americanization process. Although desiring education for their children, Catholics nonetheless found these religious practices repugnant. And they sought relief in several ways. Some asked that their children be excused from the exercises. Others petitioned for the right to read from Catholic Bible translations. Such requests to the Philadelphia authorities in the 1840's produced riots, more than a score of deaths, and the destruction of Irish immigrant homes and Catholic churches. Still others sought public funds for Catholic schools, since the institutions teaching Protestant viewpoints were so financed. But all to no avail. Even the courts refused relief, for Protestants were easily persuaded that it was a Roman Catholic plot to eliminate the Bible from the schools and weaken the Republic itself. The only solution seemed to be private Catholic schools financed by the Church. In this sense it appears quite accurate to describe the emergence of the parochial system as a protest against the Protestant and anti-Catholic bias in the public schools of the nineteenth century.[9]

The first provincial council of seven Catholic bishops was held in Baltimore in 1829. Noting the dangers involved in public school attendance, the bishops urged upon Catholics the necessity of starting their own institutions. The fourth and fifth councils, in 1840 and 1843, repeated this observation and advice. The First Plenary Council, held in 1852, ordered pastors to teach doctrine to the

---

[9] Neil G. McCluskey, *Catholic Viewpoint on Education,* rev. ed. (Garden City, New York: Doubleday & Company, Inc., 1962), pp. 12–13.

[10] Gerard S. Sloyan, "Roman Catholic Religious Education," in *Religious Education: A Comprehensive Survey op. cit.,* pp. 402–405.

young in their parishes. The Second Plenary Council, of 1866, reiterated the injunction about parish schools and added catechetical instruction to the pastor's teaching of the children remaining in public schools. The Third Plenary Council (1884) issued no exhortations. It decreed. Each church was given only two years to comply with the parish school edict, and only a bishop under exceptional circumstances could postpone compliance. Catholic parents were ordered to send their children to the church's schools. These instructions were concerned only with elementary schools, and the people moved quickly to comply.

The twentieth century has witnessed a similar emphasis upon secondary education within Catholicism. In 1900 most boys who received a Catholic education attended the preparatory departments of church colleges, and girls were in private academies maintained by religious orders. But by 1911 the National Catholic Educational Association was urging parish and diocesan high schools as the obvious upward extension of the elementary system. Philadelphia had actually opened the first such school for boys in 1890, and by 1910 the number had grown to 310, and to more than 1500 in the 1950's. Thus, once the basic decision had been made to create a private, church-supported system of schools, the Catholic citizenry worked diligently to achieve its goal. This has been no easy task, since the rapid increase in the population has compounded the problem. In many decades, even with the large number of new schools opening, the national percentage has not improved. This remains a major problem for the Catholic Church today as its constituency increases dramatically.

CHAPTER II

Religion, Morality and
The Public Schools: Legal Bases

Introduction

The proper relationship between religion and the tax-supported public schools is one of the major issues confronting the churches and the schools today. A reading of nineteenth century educational history might lead one to conclude that the questions were all resolved. The facts are quite contrary to this simple assessment, for two of the most far-reaching decisions have occurred in the 1960's. From the public clamor and controversy which erupted, it seems evident that the issues are not fully settled even by these pronouncements.

The preceding century was a time during which the role played by religion steadily changed in the public schools, moving from an excessive emphasis on Protestant sectarianism to a gradually diminishing amount of religious instruction. By the end of the century, and indeed earlier in many parts of the nation, religious involvement had been reduced to devotional exercises, Bible reading, and religious ceremonials at Christmas and Easter. And in many states most or even all of these had disappeared from the classroom. But the practices which remained were to produce conflict and litigation in this century, and the issue of legality (or constitutionality) has continued to be a living concern.

Former Justice Felix Frankfurter once wrote that "preoccupation by our people with the constitutionality, instead of with the wisdom, of legislation or executive action is preoccupation with a false value." Be that as it may, just such a preoccupation has captured American interest, and the controversies have revolved around the propriety or impropriety of any given practice in the light of the Constitution's references to religion.

The First and the Fourteenth Amendments

Religion actually plays quite a minor role in the United States Constitution. Except for a reference in Article VI forbidding any religious test for holding office, the only other reference is found in the First Amendment. This amendment is one of the ten generally known as the Bill of Rights, which were adopted soon after the federal government was established in 1789. Proposed by James Madison in March of that year and revised in a variety of ways in the ensuing six months, the adopted amendment read partially: "Congress shall make no law respecting an establishment of religion, or prohibiting the free exercise thereof." The remaining sections of the amendment granted similar guarantees on freedom of speech, press, and right to assemble peaceably. It should be noted that its provisions apply only to the Congress. Though Madison intended, and the House of Representatives agreed, that the several states should be included, the Senate declined and Congress alone was thus enjoined.

The language is simple enough, but its meaning has proved to be much more complex. In response to an inquiry directed to him by the Danbury, Connecticut, Baptist Association, President Thomas Jefferson penned some now famous words, having first cleared the language with his Attorney General. He wrote that the amendment builds "a wall of separation between church and state," phraseology which many claim has clouded the issue in subsequent attempts by the courts to clarify and apply the freedoms guaranteed by the First Amendment.

The application of this amendment to actions taken by the states (rather than the federal government) was delayed for many years. As a part of the post-Civil War efforts to safeguard civil rights, the Fourteenth Amendment was adopted in 1868. It reads (in part): "No State shall make or enforce any law which shall abridge the privileges or immunities of citizens of the United States; nor shall any State deprive any person of life, liberty, or property, without due process of law; nor deny to any person within its jurisdiction the equal protection of the laws." Thus, Madison's intent of 80 years earlier was finally realized by this action, and the central government became an active defender—against the states, if necessary—of those rights which had been originally conferred in the Bill of Rights. It is not surprising to find that the utilization of these amendments in relation to religion and public education has frequently been in the federal courts, and this despite the fact that educational law has been a matter reserved almost exclusively to the states by the Constitution.

The first instance of this application, *Meyer v. Nebraska, 262*

U.S. 390, was not concerned with religion. The state of Nebraska in 1919, as a part of the Americanism fervor sweeping the country after World War I, had legislated to require that all school instruction be conducted only in English. Several Lutheran parochial schools used German, the language spoken in the homes of their students. Upon appeal the United States Supreme Court held that the liberty guaranteed in the Fourteenth Amendment had, in fact, been abridged by this state law, and the act was declared unconstitutional. Thus was set into motion a movement which was to affect the relationship between religion and education in numerous ways. A consideration of these court actions follows.[1]

The Important Judicial Decisions

Pierce v. Society of Sisters, 268 U.S. 510 (1925). In 1922 the state of Oregon, by public referendum vote, adopted a law which would have abolished all nonpublic schools. The regulation required attendance by all children between eight and sixteen years of age in public schools, with few exceptions granted—and none for religious reasons. The Catholic Society of Sisters and a private military academy filed suit against Governor Pierce to halt the law's implementation. Ultimately reaching the United States Supreme Court, the majority opinion held for the private schools and against the state. The argument actually turned on the matter of property rights rather than freedom of religion. The Court readily affirmed the right of the state to regulate all schools, private as well as public, and to set minimum standards regarding attendance. But it specifically denied to the state the right or power to require pupils to attend the public school. Justice McReynolds wrote: "The child is not the mere creature of the state; those who nurture him and direct his destiny have the right, coupled with the high duty, to recognize and prepare him for additional obligations."

Since 1925 this decision has been viewed as the Magna Carta for all private schools. Protestant, Catholic, Jewish and nonreligious private schools have found in it their charter for existence. It has meant that religious groups, which for varying reasons may be unhappy with the religiously neutral public school, may establish parallel institutions as direct substitutes. Their only obligation

---

[1] R. Freeman Butts, *The American Tradition in Religion and Education* (Boston: Beacon Press, Inc., 1950), pp. 68–145; and Richard B. Dierenfield, *Religion in American Public Schools* (Washington, D.C.: Public Affairs Press, 1962), pp. 1–25.

is to meet all minimum standards erected by the state, and once this is done religion may be taught without question.

Cochran v. Board of Education, 281 U.S. 370 (1930). The validity of the private religious school having been determined by the Pierce case, the next issue was indirect support for such enterprises. Louisiana provided the vehicle for interpretation. Although the state constitution specifically prohibited use of public funds for sectarian schools, a Louisiana law made these funds available for purchase of textbooks for all pupils, regardless of schools attended. A citizen, Cochran by name, challenged this in the state courts on the ground that he was being taxed to support sectarian religion. By a 3–2 decision the state supreme court held against him. On appeal the United States Supreme Court unanimously agreed both with the lower court ruling and its logic. Chief Justice Hughes wrote: "The [parochial] schools, however, are not the beneficiaries of these appropriations. They obtain nothing from them, nor are they relieved of a single obligation, because of them. The school children and the state alone are the beneficiaries." He added that no religious texts were involved. The books being purchased were the purely secular volumes used in public and private schools alike. The rationale of this decision has sometimes been called the "child-benefit theory." The Court saw nothing in the federal Constitution, the First, or the Fourteenth Amendments which would prohibit such welfare benefits to school children in any school. It must be understood that the decision is permissive only, not mandatory. It *permits* a state whose constitution concurs to purchase nonreligious textbooks for all pupils. It *does not require* it.

Everson v. Board of Education, 330 U.S. 1 (1947). The same legal principle arose again over bus transportation. Several states provided transportation to both public and parochial schools at public expense. When challenged in the courts, the case ultimately reached the United States Supreme Court. Here, by a narrow 5–4 decision, the majority reaffirmed the Cochran decision, and the practice was sustained—again on a permissive basis. But both the majority and minority opinions introduced a new element for the first time. This was a consideration of the meaning of the "establishment" clause in the First Amendment. Justice Black wrote (for the majority): "Neither a state nor the federal government can set up a church. Neither can pass laws which aid one religion, aid all religions, or prefer one religion over another." The majority found no violation here in bus transportation. Justice Rutledge disagreed.

He saw the prohibition in the establishment clause as broadly forbidding "state support, financial or other, of religion in any guise, form or degree. It outlaws all use of public funds for religious purposes." Justice Jackson agreed, in saying: "The prohibition against establishment of religion cannot be circumvented by a subsidy, bonus or reimbursement of expense to individuals for receiving religious instruction and indoctrination. . . ." The introduction of the First Amendment into these deliberations doubtless played a role in the very close decision.

Since 1947 the matter has not been clarified very much. As recently as 1962 the Oregon Supreme Court rejected the logic of the child-benefit or welfare theory and disallowed textbooks for all pupils. The Oregon court specifically stated its acceptance of the Everson's minority position, and the United States Supreme Court refused to review the decision. Thus, substantial opposition continues, and its effect shall be noted below in the consideration of federal aid to parochial schools. The critics of Cochran–Everson see the decisions as an oblique breaching of the separation principle. Their proponents, of course, are unwilling to accept the logic of strict separation.[2]

McCollum v. Board of Education, 333 U.S. 203 (1948). The next important court case moved directly into the matter of religion in the public school; not in the curriculum, but rather in the building. Weekday or released-time religious education developed steadily after its appearance in 1914. State practices varied, since there was no national organizing agency providing over-all guidance. And state court decisions regarding its legality tended to fall on both sides, although the trend up to 1948 appeared favorable. The Champaign, Illinois, program became the focal point for ultimate decision. There public school children were released from their regular curriculum for classes held in the school building and taught by clergymen or other church personnel. Mrs. Vashti McCollum, a professed atheist, appealed for relief through the state courts and finally to the United States Supreme Court. After full hearing, the Court decided by an 8–1 vote that the practice was untenable. Justice Black wrote for the eight-man majority:

> The foregoing facts . . . show the use of tax-supported property for religious instruction and the close cooperation between the school authorities and the religious council in promoting religious education.

[2] Robert F. Drinan, *Religion, the Courts and Public Policy* (New York: McGraw-Hill Book Company, 1963), pp. 136–160.

The operation of the State's compulsory education system thus assists and is integrated with the program of religious instruction carried on by separate religious sects. Pupils compelled by law to go to school for secular education are released in part from their legal duty upon the condition that they attend the religious classes. This is beyond all question a utilization of the tax-established and tax-supported public school system to aid religious groups to spread their faith. And it falls squarely under the ban of the First Amendment (made applicable to the States by the Fourteenth) as we interpreted it in Everson v. Board of Education, 330 U.S. 1.

Thus, two points were crucial: use of school buildings, and use of school authorities in getting pupils into classes via release.

Public response was instant and strong; few approved, almost all condemned. Many presumed this to be the death of all released-time programs, regardless of their specific characteristics. And a St. Louis court so ruled, holding that even classes meeting outside the school property fell under McCollum's ban.[3] But such was not to be the opinion of the United States Supreme Court's majority, as indicated in the next case.

Zorach v. Clauson, 343 U.S. 306 (1952). Some released-time programs were halted after McCollum, but others sought to avoid the illegalities identified therein. In New York City, for example, classes were held away from school property, and the school authorities gave little or no assistance to the administration of the instruction. When challenged, the practice reached the United States Supreme Court where a 6–3 majority found it to be substantially different from that in McCollum. Some have held that this represents a retreat on the part of the Court from the clear-cut principle laid down in McCollum. This seems to be the major substance of the minority dissents. But it appears equally reasonable to hold, with the majority, that Zorach is actually affirming McCollum. Two important objections were raised to the Champaign pattern. Both were missing from New York City's classes, and the Court was consistent in relation to McCollum while allowing New York City to continue its program. As Dierenfield's study revealed, the McCollum decision has been widely disobeyed, particularly in the South where about 10 per cent of the schools still permit Bible classes to be a regular part of the program. The classes are taught, in many instances, by persons employed and paid by the churches.[4] Thus,

---

[3] *Ibid.,* pp. 72–89.
[4] Dierenfield, *op. cit.,* pp. 50–53.

what the Court has decreed to be the law of the land has some decade and a half later not yet become the practice of the land!

Engel v. Vitale, 370 U.S. 421 (1962). Ten years after Zorach the legal basis for religion's relationship with education took another major step. In this instance the matter was not peripheral, since the practice called into question was central and led by regular school personnel. Being concerned about the moral education of students, the New York State Board of Regents in 1951 issued a "Statement on Moral and Spiritual Training in the Schools," including a brief prayer which read as follows: "Almighty God, we acknowledge our dependence upon Thee, and we beg Thy blessings upon us, our parents, our teachers and our country." The use of the prayer was to be voluntary. No classroom teacher was compelled to use it, nor was a child to be required to participate. He could be excused from the room or remain silent without penalty. Five Nassua County, Long Island, parents objected, and the courts received the case. In the New York state courts they lost, the chief judge of the Court of Appeals clearly rejecting the idea that the establishment clause was related to the matter. But such was not the case before the United States Supreme Court. After hearing arguments in the 1961–62 session on June 25, 1962, Justice Black speaking for the majority held the practice to be in violation of the establishment clause in that it introduced a religious activity. And he said, "It is no part of the business of government to compose official prayers for any group of the American people to recite as a part of a religious program carried on by government." Taking cognizance of the fact that the exercise was supposedly voluntary (a condition that many opponents were not willing to admit, since it was administered by the teacher and therefore placed the child at somewhat of a disadvantage with her and his classmates), Black indicated that this was really irrelevant. Establishment was the important point. "When the power, prestige, and financial support of government is placed behind a particular religious belief, the indirect coercive pressure upon religious minorities to conform to the prevailing officially approved religion was plain," he added. The lone dissenter, Justice Stewart, claimed that the Court had gone too far and had uncritically accepted Jefferson's metaphor regarding "a wall of separation." Rather than being an official religion, he saw only an attempt at permitting children to share in their heritage in the nation.

The response was explosive. The few voices raised in agreement went largely unheard. Criticisms were voiced by such persons as former Presidents Eisenhower and Hoover, Cardinal Spellman, and countless Congressmen and clergy. With the passage of the summer months, a more reasoned response began to be heard. Many persons came to the Court's support, but this did not impede the filing of more than 100 resolutions in Congress for the express purpose of voiding the decision.[5] But the Court had not finished. Two other equally far-reaching cases remained to be considered.

Abington School District v. Schempp and *Murray v. Curlett, 374 U.S. 203 (1963).* At the time the New York Regents prayer was being considered the Court also had under advisement appeals from Pennsylvania and Maryland involving similar but varying practices. In Pennsylvania it was Bible reading, without comment, at the beginning of each day, a custom that Dierenfield had found in 42 per cent of school systems. An earlier survey had revealed the extent of differences regarding Bible reading. In 1956 12 states required it, 12 more specifically permitted it, and another 13 permitted such readings either by silence of statutes or by their constitutions. In contrast, 11 states specifically forbade Bible reading.[6] Thus, the Pennsylvania case had widespread application across the nation. In Baltimore, Maryland, the school board, since 1905, had required the daily reading of the Bible and/or recitation of the Lord's Prayer. Both suits reached the Court at approximately the same time and were joined for judicial review and decision. It should be noted that both Pennsylvania and Baltimore amended their regulations to permit individual exemption from participation, these changes instituted while the cases were in the lower courts, an obvious attempt to neutralize criticisms which were anticipated in the high court. And in the oral arguments attorneys for both governments sought to show the moral value of the practices and diminish or erase opposition to them as religious exercises.

Speaking for the eight-member majority, Justice Clark pointed to the 1962 *Engel v. Vitale* ruling, and, reaffirming its logic, he applied the reasoning to Bible reading and the Lord's Prayer. "The place of religion in our society is an exalted one, achieved through a long tradition of reliance on the home, the church and the inviolable citadel of the individual heart and mind. We have come

---

[5] For a summary of the response see Paul Blanshard, *Religion and the Schools* (Boston: Beacon Press, Inc., 1963), pp. 27–95.

[6] Don Conway, "Religion and Public Education in the States," *International Journal of Religious Education*, XXXII (March, 1956), 34–40.

to recognize through bitter experience that it is not within the power of government to invade that citadel. . . ."

Thus, the full course has apparently been run. Beginning with Colonial schools which were not only religious but distinctly sectarian, the practice had steadily shifted toward a nonsectarian nature, and in many places this meant only Bible reading without any additional teaching by way of comment and prayer. Now the Supreme Court has ruled that even this is unconstitutional in the public schools of the land.

Unresolved Questions

The Meaning of the First Amendment. Critics of the Court as well as its friends remain uncertain about the meaning of the establishment and free exercise clauses. One argument holds that the 1962 and 1963 decisions were radical acceptances of the Jeffersonian "wall" theory, and many are unhappy with such an interpretation. They see in these rulings an expansion of the establishment clause far beyond its original intent. If the "no aid to religion" position stands, this appears to be tantamount to an establishment of official secularism. Justice Clark was careful to deny this, but critics nonetheless see it as the inevitable result of an expurgation of all religious exercises from schools. When religion is out, this "carries with it the overtones of rejection."[7] Thus, proponents of religion will doubtless press for new interpretations of the First Amendment which do not result in this alleged hostility toward religion.

Teaching ABOUT Religion. Little noticed in the public clamor after the 1963 pronouncement was one section at the conclusion of Justice Clark's opinion. He wrote:

> In addition, it might well be said that one's education is not complete without a study of comparative religion or the history of religion and its relationship to the advancement of civilization. It certainly may be said that the Bible is worthy of study for its literary and historic qualities. Nothing we have said here indicates that such study of the Bible or of religion, when presented objectively as part of a secular program of education, may not be effected consistent with the First Amendment.

Both Justices Brennan and Goldberg in their separate concurring

---

[7] Joseph Tussman, *The Supreme Court on Church and State* (New York: Oxford University Press, 1962), pp. xiii–xxiv.

opinions said substantially the same thing. Thus, in the midst of a decision widely acclaimed as the final step in the expulsion of religion from the public school, one can find a clear and unmistakeable declaration that said schools *can* teach *about* religion! Indeed, they not only can, but both Justice Clark and Justice Brennan indicate their conviction that a school which does not is doing less than a complete job. The only qualifications are that it must be taught objectively as a regular part of the curriculum, and, finally, not be a devotional exercise.

Is this feasible? Will it adequately compensate for Bible reading and prayers which must be abandoned? No one knows as yet. The question remains unresolved in early 1965. But at least two states have indicated a willingness to experiment within the framework of this newly defined permissibility. Both Florida and California have taken the initial steps toward implementing programs for teaching about religion in the regular curriculums of their public schools. Other states will doubtless follow in additional experimentation.

Shared Time Programs. The final "unresolved question" concerns the shared time experiments. Based on the premise that a parent has the legal right to determine the place of a child's education—so long as it meets minimum standards—shared time involves simultaneous dual enrollment in a private religious school and the public school. This would break the current pattern of forcing total enrollment in one school or the other. Such dual attendance would permit taking certain religiously neutral subjects (industrial arts, mathematics, physical education, some sciences,) in the public school, while taking on a complementary schedule other value-oriented courses in the religious school. The sum of the two programs would be a complete education. Both would be required to meet all state requirements, and administration of the total would be shared by the two institutions.

Proponents see this as avoiding the federal constitutional hurdle. And it enables a church, any church which is willing to pay the price for quality instruction, to inject the religious dimension into the pupils' total educational experience, an impossibility in the light of the decisions reviewed earlier in this chapter. It would also expose all students to some public school relationships, however limited. Critics, on the other hand, point out that it may be illegal, since churches that operate schools would be relieved of a portion of their current burden of finances, and this is an indirect aid to religion. All such comments are speculative, of course, since no court has ruled on the practice.

While the debate proceeds on feasibility and wisdom, experiments continue to appear. Michigan reported 50 programs during the 1963–64 school year. Pennsylvania, Missouri, Illinois, and other states were similarly engaged. The 1960's will doubtless provide more data on some of the aspects of this idea; feasibility, legality, advantages, and disadvantages. For the present it appears to be one possible, though only partial, solution to the problems regarding the legal aspects of religion's relation to the public schools.[8]

In conclusion, Justice Douglas, in his Zorach decision, wrote:

> We are a religious people whose institutions presuppose a Supreme Being. We guarantee the freedom to worship as one chooses. We make room for as wide a variety of beliefs and creeds as the spiritual needs of man deem necessary. We sponsor an attitude on the part of government that shows no partiality to any one group and that lets each flourish according to the zeal of its adherents and the appeal of its dogma.

Just what this means has not been finally settled to the satisfaction of many citizens. Some see in the Court's decisions our highest expressions of religious freedom. Others are equally convinced that these rulings have been harmful to religion. At least in a considerable portion of the public mind the issues remain unresolved.

---

[8] For the best summary of these experiments, see *Dual Enrollment in Public and Nonpublic Schools,* A Bulletin of the Bureau of Educational Research and Development, United States Office of Education (Washington, D.C.: U.S. Government Printing Office, 1965). Nine programs in five different states are described in detail.

CHAPTER III

Moral and Character Education in the Public Schools

Introduction

Character and morality have always been important goals in American education. As observed in Chapter I, during the Colonial period this generally took the form of explicit religious instruction. The nineteenth century was a transitional era which sought to retain these goals while avoiding the conflicts precipitated by sectarian divisions. The initial solution proposed was a common core of religious beliefs shared by all sects, and Bible reading without comment was the chief means employed. Jewish, Catholic, and even some Protestant objections were quickly raised, and these have also been noted. The fact that Bible reading endured for so many decades is probably explained by the extent of Protestantism's dominance in the nineteenth century. Only gradually was there a recognition of the fact that a commonly shared Protestant position was itself sectarian in nature and thus objectionable to a considerable segment of Americans.

The second attempted resolution of this dilemma was the effort to identify and teach moral values apart from any specific or particularistic theological context. Such character traits as sincerity, honesty, loyalty, courage, kindness, and the like were to be taught without reference to any body of religious belief or institution. Those who supported this view claimed that teachers could exemplify these values and build them into the personalities of their students without fear of criticism or of offending any particular group. Thus, a kind of nondenominational morality would become central for the schools. By the turn of the twentieth century there were several theories as to the best manner for accomplishing this objective.

One group of educators found the best resource in those studies generally called the humanities. They believed that the languages and literature of ancient Rome and Greece, philosophy, the fine arts, and other subjects in this area were best designed to discipline the students' intellectual faculties and develop their moral and spiritual capacities. While most influential at the higher education level, the "faculty psychology premise" can also be found in the work of William T. Harris and other writers of the late nineteenth century.[1] This classical humanism, while nontheistic in avowed foundation, was not unrelated to the sectarian positions of a century earlier.

But other competing philosophies of human nature and education were arising simultaneously. The pragmatic theories of Charles S. Peirce were being explored and popularized by William James and adapted to educational thought by John Dewey. In many ways America's greatest and most influential educational philosopher, Dewey reacted against the faculty psychology and formal discipline approaches which were prevalent. He saw education as being both a moral and social process related to the larger community in which the child's total experience occurs. His *Moral Principles in Education* developed a theory of ethics and morality which pervaded all of his educational writings.

Dewey and his contemporaries thus set a motif and sanction for moral and character emphases within public education which escaped the earlier dilemmas. And educators, especially between the two World Wars, turned increasingly to their implementation in school programs. As early as 1895 the National Education Association had recognized the need for moral education.[2] Various organizations devoted to this goal quickly appeared, including the International Committee on Moral Instruction and Training in Schools, the Character Development League of New York City, and the Character Education Institution, among others. By 1918 the director of the National Institute for Moral Instruction could report to the annual NEA meeting that more than 48 state and local plans for character education in the schools had been submitted to his organization for appraisal and evaluation. Each was to be studied and subjected to experimental verification in a normal

---

[1] Contrasting treatments of Harris' philosophy and influence are found in R. Freeman Butts & Lawrence A. Cremin, *A History of Education in American Culture* (New York: Holt, Rinehart & Winston, Inc. 1953), pp. 331–333, 343–347; and Neil G. McCluskey, *Public Schools and Moral Education* (New York: Columbia University Press, 1958), pp. 145–176.

[2] Report of the Committee of Fifteen on Elementary Education, *Proceedings of the National Education Association, XXXIV* (Washington, D.C.: National Education Association, 1895), 312.

school program.[3] The continued and increasing interest in character education is further reflected by an examination of the Tenth Yearbook issued by the NEA's Department of Superintendence. Entitled *Character Education,* the volume included chapters on such topics as "Theory of Character Education," "Objectives of Character Education," "Character Education and the Curriculum," "The Teacher in Character Education," and so on.[4] Even a casual check of publications in the 1920's and early 1930's reveals scores of volumes devoted to the implementation of specific plans for moral and character education. One of the better known was Charters' *The Teaching of Ideals.*[5] After developing a theory of traits and ideals of character which were held desirable, Charters presented a program for direct and indirect instruction designed to produce their implantation in the personality of school pupils. His scheme involved the use of the life situation of the school, rewards and punishments, the role of the teaching, varieties of teaching-learning functions, and a system for measuring results. McKown's analysis of this movement is a fascinating survey of the many ways that public education sought to live up to its responsibilities for character development.[6]

But the emphasis did not last. Subjected to searching scrutiny, character education programs were found wanting by many researchers. The "Character Education Inquiry" is an illustration. Through an intricate and clever series of tests the inquiry examined the traits which schools were seeking to develop but found little evidence that generalized traits do in fact exist. A given child often varied from situation to situation, tending to be honest, for example, in one and dishonest in another. There was little apparent transfer from one to the other or from the general to the specific.[7] This and numerous other similar researches tended to bring into serious question almost all of the programs for moral and character education existing in the late 1920's and 1930's. The result was a rather rapid

[3] Milton Fairchild, "Character Education," *Addresses and Proceedings of the National Education Association,* LVI (1918), 120–122.

[4] *Character Education,* Tenth Yearbook of the Department of Superintendence (Washington, D.C.: National Education Association, 1932).

[5] W. W. Charters, *The Teaching of Ideals* (New York: The MacMillan Company, 1928).

[6] Harry C. McKown, *Character Education* (New York: McGraw-Hill Book Company, 1935).

[7] Hugh Hartshorne, *et al., Studies in Deceit* (New York: The Macmillan Company, 1928); *Studies in Service and Self Control* (New York: The Macmillan Company, 1929); and *Studies in the Organization of Character* (New York: The Macmillan Company, 1930).

moving away from the popular courses and programs which had been designed to develop specific character traits. And this was the prevailing situation as the years of the fourth decade drew to a close.

A Survey of Major Recent Publications
on Moral and Character Education Theory

Public education could not escape the crises of the 1930's and 1940's any more easily than the remainder of American society. The great depression was a crisis in economic values with strong overtones of morality. And World War II quickly followed it, and in some respects was responsible for its passing. The war itself was a crisis in moral and spiritual values. Thus, educators could not be content with a repudiation of responsibility based on the inadequacy of former theories of value education. So once again influential individuals and educational organizations turned their attention to the tasks of the public schools and their adequacy for this role. It is impossible to survey more than a few samples of this work, but three which are representative and proved to be important have been selected.

The first to appear was the Seventh Yearbook of the John Dewey Society. This group of educators regularly concentrated its scholarly studies on crucial issues facing American education. In early 1943 when the book was being planned, none was more crucial than the need to recognize and support spiritual values. A committee of eight prepared the manuscript which identified the essential spiritual values as "moral insight, integrity of thought and act, equal regard for human personality wherever found, faith in the free play of intelligence both to guide study and to direct action; and, finally, those further values of refined thought and feeling requisite to bring life to its finest quality."[8] It was the committee's premise that these values are not inborn but acquired, and their acquisition is a major purpose for which schools exist. And it added, not only is the school potentially capable of doing this, but "it can do it on the basis of human reason and experience and without necessary recourse to religious authority." Thus, the historic separation of church and state was sustained while simultaneously permitting the school freedom to teach these spiritual values. The report claimed the schools

---

[8] John S. Brubacher (ed.), *The Public Schools and Spiritual Values,* Seventh Yearbook of the John Dewey Society (New York: Harper & Row, Publishers, 1944), p. 2.

had no exclusive right to teach these values. It was a shared responsibility with the religious groups, and in fact one chapter (not representative of total committee thinking) specifically defined the
religious dimension of these values. But the basic thrust of the report
was secular. It saw the public school as the common school legally
separate from any religious sanctions, and it proposed the development of these values from this secular perspective. The yearbook
served the important function of calling educators back again to a
task which had dominated their thinking twenty years earlier but
which more recently had been neglected.

The next statement to be considered is the 1947 pronouncement
by the American Council on Education's Committee on Religion
and Education. Created in early 1944 the committee had diligently
studied the subject of the interrelationship between religion and education, as well as proposals for the inclusion of moral and spiritual
values in the public schools. Its report[9] constituted not only a declaration of position, but also a critique of the existing thinking and
practice. In some ways it stands as a response to the John Dewey
Society yearbook noted above.

Reflecting upon the process of secularization, the committee concluded that it had gone too far. Noting that some persons find secularism to be a way of life, the committee rejected this position as
being unrepresentative of Americans generally. And it concluded
that the complete elimination of religion from public education was
an extreme unnecessary from legal requirements and unwise from
the viewpoint of the child's total educational development. Its exclusion implies a duality about religion and the rest of life which
leads inevitably to the conclusion that religious education is at best
only marginal and unimportant. And further, the committee added,
it seems to make religion so remote from life that no integration
with general education seems necessary. These trends the committee
proposed to reverse.

Before making positive proposals, however, the committee was
careful to point out what it didn't suggest. These educators were
opposed to all sectarian instruction and to the popular notion that
pluralistic Americans could arrive at some shared common core of
religious belief which could be taught. Neither alternative was acceptable to the committee. The members heartily approved of the

---

[9] American Council on Education, Committee on Religion and Education, *The
Relation of Religion to Public Education: The Basic Principles* (Washington, D.C.:
The Council, 1947).

current emphasis upon moral and spiritual values, but they concluded that this was inadequate. Moral and spiritual values do not
represent the "full and valid content of religion." Religion assumes
a personal identification with the ultimate source of values and faith
in their validity. This was not envisaged by the John Dewey Society
proposals or other similar ones. So, the committee concluded that,
while moral and spiritual value programs were important, by themselves they were inadequate. Something more was needed if the
public school was to measure up to its challenge.

The additional element proposed by the committee was the objective study of religious values characteristic of the various faiths
and the full treatment of religion at whatever points it naturally occurs in literature, music and the fine arts, history, social studies, and
other regular subjects of the curriculum. This would extend the curriculum to include religion just as it already comprehends other
aspects of the culture. By ignoring religion the schools had been
denying students the opportunity to learn about it. A reversal of this
policy would help to overcome the prevailing religious illiteracy and
make possible an intelligent understanding of the role that religion
has had in our culture. And, further, it would bring about a positive
appreciation for religion, from which position informed responses to
its claims might be made. This presupposed, the committee clearly
admitted, a philosophy which holds that education is incomplete un-
less it results in convictions and actions worthy of one's choices.
They concluded by illustrating ways that this might be implemented
in the curriculum of schools at various levels and its relationship to
home, church, and community.

The responses were predictable. Strong separationists and those
committed to a secular philosophy of life claimed that it was illegal.
But an even more serious objection posed was the possibility that
such a proposal opened the door to all sorts of sectarian indoctrination masked under the guise of "objective study." Others, chiefly
churchmen, saw in the proposal an answer to their major single
problem in the continued support of the public school. But some
religious leaders, who could be content with nothing less than the
wedding of particularistic religious instruction with the balance of
general education, concluded that it was an unwise, unsatisfactory
compromise.

The final volume to be considered here is the National Education
Association's publication from its Educational Policies Commission
entitled *Moral and Spiritual Values in the Public Schools*. Issued in

1951 it was the result of a three-year investigation regarding ways to improve the teaching of moral and spiritual values. The report agreed with the American Council on Education regarding teaching religious content wherever it was appropriate to the subject matter, but its most significant aspect concerned the moral and spiritual value emphasis. After a preamble designed to lay a foundation for such a program, the document identified ten important values: the basic value of human personality, moral responsibility, institutions as men's servants, common consent, devotion to truth, respect for excellence, moral equality, brotherhood, the pursuit of happiness, and spiritual enrichment.[10] Various sanctions or reasons for acceptance of the values are considered, none of which violates the church-state separation concept. The report concludes its discussion of school policy by identifying at least nine ways by which educational institutions can actively promote acquisition of these values. It also sought to set the school in proper relation to other community agencies with value formation responsibility, such as, the home and religious institutions.

Public reaction was not greatly different from that afforded the American Council statement. A midsummer, 1951 issue of the journal, *Religious Education*, perhaps illustrates this best. Fifteen prominent persons in education, including representatives from the three major faith groups, were asked to evaluate the report. Their responses ranged from clear-cut support to veiled and even open criticism. Especially criticized was the report's support of the teaching of religious content.[11]

The responses to all of these statements can be summarized in the same way. General agreement existed regarding the crisis in the lack of moral values in the educational program and this extended to the proposition that the schools had some responsibility regarding its alleviation. But divergencies of opinion emerged immediately when specific programs were proposed. The conflict was sharpest precisely at the point where values and religion appeared to be related and correspondingly lessened where religion was not a factor.

A recent report by the American Association of School Administrators has sought to clarify both the legal and the cultural obligations facing the public schools. Prepared by its Commission on

---

[10] Educational Policies Commission, *Moral and Spiritual Values in the Public Schools* (Washington, D.C.: National Education Association, 1951).

[11] See symposium on *Moral and Spiritual Values in the Public Schools*, in *Religious Education*, XLVI (July–August, 1951), 195–236.

Religion in the Public Schools, the document[12] explores America's heritage of religious commitment, the judicial restraints (See Chapter II), and the traditional school practices. The authors trod a careful middle-of-the-road path, urging on the one hand full acceptance of the recent United States Supreme Court decisions but on the other the honest recognition of religion's importance. The report is a well-balanced set of guidelines for public school administrators.

Some Representative Programs

Despite this mixed response to the theory of moral and spiritual values in the schools, the practical response was tremendous. Almost everyone agreed that the public schools did have an obligation in the character development of their pupils, and the post-World War II programs for implementing this conviction have been numerous. An illustration of this is the reply to Dierenfield's questionnaires. More than 99 per cent of respondents readily included the teaching of moral values in their aims and objectives, and 77 per cent reported supplying specific materials to classroom teachers to assist in reaching these goals. The prevalence of spiritual value emphasis was somewhat lower, but still significant. More than 78 per cent accepted responsibility and 46 per cent made materials available.[13] This widespread interest was further revealed by the American Council on Education's survey conducted in the early 1950's. The Committee on Religion and Education found many state departments of instruction with bulletins outlining recommended programs, and a large number of cities had conducted their own studies and written manuals for teachers and administrators.[14] An examination of two of these state programs will demonstrate their nature and purposes.

The Kentucky experiment began in the 1940's in response to the same needs which motivated other states. An initial committee prepared a statement on "Guiding Principles" and suggested approaches. It defined moral and spiritual education as

> . . . that phase of the school program which seeks to help growing persons to achieve an understanding of their relations to nature and

---

[12] *Religion in the Public Schools* (Washington, D.C.: American Association of School Administrators, 1964).

[13] Richard B. Dierenfield, *Religion in American Public Schools* (Washington, D.C.: Public Affairs Press, 1962), pp. 45–48.

[14] Committee on Religion and Education, *The Function of the Public Schools in Dealing with Religion* (Washington, D.C.: American Council on Education, 1953), pp. 127–145.

society, to discover the moral and spiritual nature of these relations and the moral obligations involved in them in the light of the growing moral and spiritual values which man has tested through centuries of living and which are recorded in his cultural traditions, to learn to control their conduct by these standards, and to achieve a philosophy of life.[15]

The proposal maintained a clear separation between church and state, keeping both general theological and sectarian instruction apart from the schools. These moral and spiritual qualities were believed to be present in all kinds of living experience, as opposed to the earlier tendency to define them as abstract or generalized traits. Thus, such qualities need not be injected into the school from the outside by church or other group, for they are inherent in all of the relations and activities of the school and a part of every normal teaching-learning situation. The task of the school was defined as helping the pupil identify the value components in his experiences and learn from the choices which he is called upon to make. The teacher's role is that of providing guidance and counsel in the discovery and development of those situations in the total school program which are value laden. This does not involve an additional course or subject; it rather comprises an emphasis which should permeate the entire institution's life. But, since no student's life can be isolated from his nonschool experiences, the program requires active understanding and cooperation from all community agencies which influence him. This complete philosophy has been best described by William Clayton Bower, chairman of the advisory committee which produced it.[16]

Once the basic philosophy had been established, Kentucky arranged for review and criticism by school superintendents and teacher-education specialists. Pilot locales for experimentation were selected, and representatives from these schools engaged in an extensive study to identify approaches and materials which might be useful. Six school systems actually began the experiments in September, 1949. Their efforts were evaluated in workshops in the summer of 1950 and strengthened plans tried in the same schools during 1950–51. At the same time it was concluded that a program of sufficient clarity and defensibility had been achieved to permit

---

15 Department of Education, Commonwealth of Kentucky, *Moral and Spiritual Values in Education,* Educational Bulletin XVII (Frankfort: Department of Education, January 1950), p. 978.

16 William Clayton Bower, *Moral and Spiritual Values in Education* (Lexington: University of Kentucky Press, 1952), pp. 27–89.

extension to other systems throughout the state. Several workshops were held in 1951 and subsequent summers to which any interested public school personnel was invited. And the program continues on this optional basis; recommended by the state department of education, supported financially and with guidance materials and staff members, and available to any local school which desires to participate.[17]

Although the Kentucky program was developed independently of the study and investigation which produced the NEA's Educational Policies Commission report, it certainly parallels that document in basic philosophy and implementation. And Hartford's evaluation of the experience across the state indicates that this position is feasible and workable.

The state of California had a similar experience regarding this aspect of the school's task. As early as 1949 educators were realizing their unfulfilled responsibilities for moral and spiritual values, and the California Committee for the Study of Education appointed a group of its members to study the topic. Surveys of actual programs or individual efforts were made and published for general suggestive value. Further subcommittees continued the research and began publishing their findings. The major document is a Teacher's Guide for *Developing Moral-Spiritual Values in the Schools,*[18] available to educators who wish to implement its ideas in their work. The report includes a statement of philosophy or guiding principles which is quite similar to the Kentucky and Educational Policies Commission statements. It identifies the classroom experiences which are most fruitful for these emphases and suggests a school program to administrators. It concludes with evaluative procedures which will prove helpful to those who may wish to measure the effectiveness of moral-spiritual value emphases in their work.

A final facet for attention here concerns a major problem which most state and local programs have encountered. Few schools where the teaching of moral and spiritual values was undertaken found teachers who were competent for the task. Thus, the preparation of teachers became the focus for additional study. Various higher education groups have been interested, but the American Association of Colleges for Teacher Education performed the most productive

---

[17] For full details on the Kentucky program see Ellis Ford Hartford, *Moral Values in Public Education* (New York: Harper & Row, Publishers, 1958).

[18] *Developing Moral-Spiritual Values in the Schools* (San Francisco: Fearon Publishers, 1957).

service. As early as the mid-1940's it was surveying the role of religion in its institutions, and a preliminary report in 1947 revealed the complexity of the situation. In 1953 it appointed a Committee on Teacher Education and Religion to engage in a five-year study project designed to shed illumination on the problems and, hopefully, point the way toward their solutions. The committee's report appeared in 1959.[19] The published document provides both a selective survey and some prescriptions or recommendations. It examines what has been happening on many campuses and reports these in an initial chapter. It then considers the possibilities in the four curricular divisions: professional education, the humanities, the social sciences, and the natural sciences. Concluding chapters record certain techniques and processes essential for an institution's adequate response to this need and the issues which remain unsettled.

Thus, the AACTE clearly accepted higher education's responsibility for preparing teachers who can provide an intelligent understanding of the role that religion has had in culture. This was essentially teaching about religion wherever and whenever it played a role intrinsic to the nature of the subject matter itself. The report was widely circulated among college faculties and has provided guidance regarding the manner by which teacher-education institutions might discharge their duty in reference to religious understandings.

In Conclusion

Chapters II and III have surveyed and analyzed the relationships between religious and moral education and the public schools. Certain conclusions now seem clear and capable of attracting at least majority consensus, if not unanimous approval.

The legal possibilities have been sharply defined. Religious exercises will not be permitted, including prayer and Bible readings, even though many school districts with community consent will doubtless continue to violate this court edict. One cannot help speculating about the moral education implications of such disregard of the "law of the land" by duly elected officials.

On the other hand the United States Supreme Court has for the first time given approval to the "study about religion" proposals found in the American Council on Education and National Educa-

---

[19] A. L. Sebaly (ed.), *Teacher Education and Religion* (Oneonta, New York: The American Association of Colleges for Teacher Education, 1959).

tion Association publications. As noted above, the Court's opinion does not merely approve. It states that education which ignores this dimension will be incomplete and inadequate. Thus, these suggestions—now more than a decade old but previously under some legal shadow—are clearly permissible. So long as teaching proceeds on the basis of objectivity public school officials may presume that such curricular concerns cannot be legally opposed. It must be noted, of course, that not every citizen in every community will think such instruction wise or desirable, and criticisms will doubtless be made of schools which do seek to implement such programs.

The Court has not been called to rule on the legality of the moral-spiritual value programs. But it can be concluded from rulings at hand that the basic goals and features of these programs are acceptable. And their need seems abundantly clear. As countless commentators have suggested, the most crucial task facing the United States may well be a restoration of proper balance between technological and scientific achievements on the one hand and cultural and moral values on the other. And the responsibility falls squarely on the schools, as well as other institutions whose claims are only voluntary. This is the major challenge which confronts the public schools today. Its legality appears certain, and its achievement will not be easy. But the school, which stands as the single most authentic interpreter of our heritage and culture, must measure up to the challenge.

CHAPTER IV

Philosophies of Religious Education

Protestant Philosophies of Education

It should be noted that the word "philosophy" appears in its plural form in this section on Protestantism. This is the inevitable consequence of the diversity which exists among those who claim the Reformation as their heritage. Just as there are many denominations, so are there numerous views on the educational process and the theory guiding it. The effort here is to sketch their scope in broad outline.

One's view of the nature of the Bible has always been central in Protestantism's educational philosophies, and this remains true today. Traditionally, especially through much of the nineteenth century in the American church school, the Bible stood at the base of the curriculum. Even when catechetical instruction was dominant, the catechism was presumed to be nothing more than a systematization of the Bible's teaching. And this question/answer form of education was utilized to facilitate the mastery of the biblical message. The Bible was accepted as the "Word of God." It was "God's Revelation." And man had only to read and come to understand it in order to hear God's message for his life. Thus, the church school could be called the Bible school without other explanation being needed. The Bible was God's book, and it was the textbook of the Christian education program. Almost all of the various forms of curriculum in the nineteenth century were designed to survey the Bible's content.

But this approach could not continue unchallenged. Various issues in biblical studies, theological analysis, and educational philosophy were emerging, and Christian education was deeply influenced by them. Biblical criticism and historical analysis were bringing into question the traditional theory of the Bible's unity and the doctrine of revelation. Liberal theology was emphasizing a new locus of authority. It no longer resided in traditional revelation but was found in man's inner experience of God and his faith in Christ. Thus, the importance of the Bible shifted from its "divine" words to its testimony regarding the faith of others. Instead of being *the source* of truth it became *a resource* for guiding life.

Taking their cues from John Dewey and others within the public education sphere, George A. Coe, William C. Bower, and others erected an "experience-centered" philosophy for religious education. Primary emphasis was placed upon growth. Coe described the content of the curriculum as "social experience" rather than the learning of biblical facts or subject matter.[1] For Bower the base of the curriculum was "experience under guidance." The curricular objective was the enrichment and control of experience.[2] To both the Bible was a means, an important means, whose value was derived from its ability to guide ongoing experience. The Bible was viewed as an account of the religious experiences and personal growth of persons past, and it became a most useful source book for those who would understand their own experiences and problems and for those who sought higher and more fruitful ways of life. Particularly in the 1920's but also into the 1930's these positions with reference to the Bible and educational philosophy prevailed among those who were influential in Protestant Christian education. *The International Curriculum Guide* was produced for use by denominations which desired to prepare curriculums based on the "experience-centered" philosophy of religious education.

It is not implied that these two extremes satisfied everyone. There were many who stood in between in varying degrees of modification. But the two positions serve to sharpen the issue for educational philosophy. As Sara Little has written:

> When revelation is equated with the words of the Bible, then the church can turn to the Bible as an objective authority, and the task of Christian education is to offer biblical instruction. When revelation centers in religious experience, then the Bible is a valuable human document to be used as a resource in teaching, and its authority is primarily subjective in nature.[3]

Among the many persons who were satisfied with neither extreme were some who sought another philosophy, one which avoided the dilemma of biblical literalism on the one hand or man-centered authority on the other. The issues were sharply defined in the 1940's

---

[1] George A. Coe, *A Social Theory of Religious Education* (New York: Charles Scribner's Sons, 1917).

[2] William C. Bower, *The Curriculum of Religious Education* (New York: Charles Scribner's Sons, 1925).

[3] Sara Little, *The Role of the Bible in Contemporary Christian Education* (Richmond, Virginia: John Knox Press, 1961), pp. 24–25.

by two authors. Elliott's *Can Religious Education Be Christian?*[4] was a pointed attack on those who would mold educational philosophy within the context of neo-orthodox theology, while Smith's *Faith and Nurture*[5] was an equally precise attack on the liberal theology which prevailed in the modern religious education movement. Although Smith's book was essentially negative in challenging a position held to be inadequate without providing any clear substitute, there was a pronounced trend toward the "reconsiderations" which he demanded. A renewed interest in the emphasis on the values in the Christian heritage can be discerned. Vieth's *The Church and Christian Education*,[6] published in 1947, clearly marked the change. Whereas there had been much emphasis on the human quest for the good life, there was now a strong affirmation of the fact that God has revealed himself in human history. The Bible, in the context of this theology, came to be viewed as the unique book which points to God's acts of redemption in history. It was presented as having an integrity of its own which Christian education was inescapably bound to present. The Bible bears witness to a faith in God which must be appropriated by the learner if the learning experience is to be distinctly Christian. Thus, for those who took Karl Barth's theology and the entire neo-orthodox movement seriously, there was a pronounced renewal of attention to the Bible and Christian theology in the curriculum of Christian education. The *Christian Faith and Life* curriculum of the United Presbyterian Church is perhaps the best known effort to construct an entire educational program on this philosophy. Other curriculum ventures in the 1950's and 1960's have also been deeply influenced by these theories.

Parallel with these emphases there has been an effort to develop an educational philosophy which avoids subject matter as its organizational principle. One criticism of the "new theology and education" has been its concern for theological content in the curriculum. Some observers have claimed that its neo-orthodox doctrine of revelation has led to an emphasis upon theological formulations and biblical information which is not different in kind from the traditional verbal literalism and inerrancy. The Cooperative Curriculum

---

4 Harrison Elliott, *Can Religious Education be Christian?* (New York: The Macmillan Company, 1940).

5 H. Shelton Smith, *Faith and Nurture* (New York: Charles Scribner's Sons, 1941).

6 Paul H. Vieth, *The Church and Christian Education* (St. Louis: Bethany Press, 1947).

Project of the National Council of Churches has pioneered in this effort to avoid exclusive emphasis upon either life needs or biblical subject matter. This exploration, plus the work of the National Council's committees on objectives, has produced the following statement on the purposes of Christian education. Its objective is defined as that of helping

> persons to be aware of God's self-disclosure and seeking love in Jesus Christ and respond in faith and love—to the end that they may know who they are and what their human situation means, grow as sons of God rooted in the Christian community, live in the Spirit of God in every relationship, fulfill their common discipleship in the world, and abide in the Christian hope.[7]

This emphasis upon the Gospel—God's self-disclosure and seeking love—is the content; it is factual and informational. But the emphasis is cast within a personal framework. The objective is not just awareness. It is also response, and the response is stated in terms of life's activities.

This philosophy has also served to guide curriculum research and planning among the denominations. As will be discussed in more detail in Chapter V, The Methodist Church's new curriculum for children, introduced in the fall of 1964, was deeply influenced by this theory in all stages of its development. And more than a dozen other denominations have been active in the Project.

In contemporary Protestant Christian education one can discern all three philosophical elements, as well as variations on them. The traditional Bible-centered philosophy prevails in conservative Protestantism (as is described in Chapter V's references to the National Sunday School Association and the National Association of Evangelicals). A recent textbook on philosophy, titled *A Christian Approach to Education,* bears the subtitle "A Bibliocentric View." Its author writes:

> The Christian curriculum begins properly with the Bible, the Word of God. . . . The Bible itself becomes the central subject in the subject matter curriculum. Since it contains the record of God's truth as inspired by the Holy Spirit . . . , it is also the basis by which all other channels of knowledge are evaluated and used.[8]

Those who accept this view usually object to the Barthian influ-

---

7 Cited by D. Campbell Wyckoff, *Theory and Design of Christian Education Curriculum* (Philadelphia: The Westminster Press, 1961), p. 46.

8 H. W. Byrne, *A Christian Approach to Education* (Grand Rapids, Michigan: Zondervan Publishing House, 1961), p. 66.

enced concepts of revelation. They see in such definitions too strong an emphasis upon the actions of God, particularly in the life and work of Christ, and too little stress on the "sayings" of God. While striving diligently to avoid earlier literalism, they insist that both what God has *said* (as contained in the Bible) and *done* must be taken together. Thus, in many ways their philosophy of Christian education is in general agreement with the nineteenth century devotion to the written words of the Bible.[9] And the curriculums developed by the denominations and publishing houses affiliated with the National Sunday School Association reflect this theory of Christian nurture.

To these conservative philosophies must be added the others identified. The pragmatic philosophy of Dewey and his followers continues to influence some Protestant curriculum theory, as does the theological position of neo-orthodoxy. Christian education within Protestantism remains diverse.

Jewish Educational Philosophies

Jewish educational philosophy can be traced to the Old Testament where, in the middle of the fifth century B.C., Ezra is reported to have read the Book of the Law to the people of Jerusalem (see Nehemiah 8). Through the centuries this reverence for the Law has prevailed, and a major facet of the practice of Judaism has centered around its systematic study. One chief goal of the righteous life is to fulfill the Law by doing the Will of God, and this Law and Will can be known only as one diligently studies the Bible and the Talmud—the authoritative interpretations of the Bible. As Louis Finkelstein has written, study is thus "far more than a pleasing intellectual exercise, and is itself a means of communion with God."[10] The Jewish doctrine of man posits his potentiality for growth toward God. But this is not merely individualistic. He can and does learn from others who have gone before. This "sacred" history has been preserved in the Scriptures, and the devout Jew gives himself to their study as a means of meeting the divine.[11]

---

[9] See Carl F. H. Henry, "Basic Issues in Modern Theology: Revelation As Truth," *Christianity Today,* IX (January 1, 1965), 14–17.

[10] Louis Finkelstein, "The Jewish Religion: Its Beliefs and Practices," in *The Jews: Their History, Culture, and Religion* (ed.) Louis Finkelstein (New York: Harper & Row, Publishers, 1949), II, 1331.

[11] Eugene B. Borowitz, "A Jewish View of Education," in *Philosophies of Education* (ed.) Philip H. Phenix (New York: John Wiley & Sons, Inc., 1961), p. 87.

American Judaism subscribes generally to this focal point for education, but this does not mean that ideological unity prevails. Today three "denominations" are in existence, and a fourth "philosophy" has numerous adherents. But such diversity is relatively recent within American Judaism, its formal structures being less than 100 years old.

Orthodoxy is the traditional rabbinic Judaism, as its name implies. It holds that both the Law and the Oral interpretations were simultaneously and uniquely revealed at Sinai. Both were authoritatively handed down through the centuries until they were incorporated in the Bible and the Talmud, the basic sources for all religious teaching. The sixteenth century *Schulkhan Arukh* (code of law) is generally accepted as a valid and accurate summary of the commands contained in these teachings. Orthodoxy insists that "Judaism is not a religion based on speculation. Its major task is not to solve the ultimate question of the nature of God. The Torah is rather the divine guidance to the right life. Jewish duty consists in the application of the Torah ideals to the hundred and one tasks of daily life."[12] Thus, if Judaism is a way of life which requires meticulous observance of the Torah precepts, Orthodoxy's education must automatically be committed to intensive study of the Scriptures in Hebrew, the original language. Only in this manner can one come to know, understand, and fulfill the many demands of the "God-directed form of life." It is this spirit within Orthodoxy which has led it to be the sponsor for most of the all-day schools (of the parochial type) and the afternoon supplementary programs which are the most complete in their scope. Bible, Talmud, prayer, ethics (the application of the code of law to daily living), and Hebrew language are central in the curriculum.

At the opposite extreme stands the *Reform* movement. Begun in Germany early in the nineteenth century, it gradually took shape in the United States from the 1860's to 1889. In essence Reform Judaism is an attempt to accommodate Jewish religion to the social, political, scientific, and cultural conditions of modern living. It is often referred to in the United States as the "Americanizing" of Judaism. Jewishness, or that which separates the Jew from others, is defined as a religion, and it stresses contemporaneity. In contrast to Orthodoxy's definition of Judaism as a way of life, Reform has emphasized theological and creedal concerns—even

---

[12] *A Model Program for the Talmud Torah* (New York: The Union of Orthodox Jewish Congregations, 1942), p. 13.

though considerable hesitation about a "Jewish theology" still exists in Reform.[13] The liturgy has been modernized, the vernacular language is used, and the theological bases of the faith have been reinterpreted. The traditional *Schulkhan Arukh* is not binding and the dietary laws are no longer observed. The scientific and modern scholarly interpretation of Scripture is fully accepted. In its educational emphasis Reform has wanted the child to grow up as a full participant in the culture of the total community, not just its Jewish segment. It has favored public school attendance and held that its basic religious educational objectives could be accomplished primarily on the weekends with some midweek instruction as a supplement. The Hebrew language is viewed as a significant part of the curriculum chiefly for an understanding of the portions of the liturgy where the original language has been retained. But all teaching is done in English, and the mastery of Hebrew is reserved for those few pupils who desire to study the language.

Conservative Judaism stands in the middle. While it does accept the authority of the Law as it has been preserved and understood in the Bible and the Talmud, Conservatism sees need for even the sacred Law to be subject to change and development. Scientific Bible study is readily accepted, and Jewish values re-examined. But, as its name implies, there is a strong tendency to conserve the traditions. The historical religious forms and traditions are retained wherever possible. In liturgy, although some vernacular prayers are used, Hebrew predominates. And the innovations which have been adopted usually represent an adaptation from some ancient practice rather than the totally new. It is claimed that any change must be defensible from the inner logic of the Law. Thus, a particular custom or practice may be altered only when the basic principle which the custom sought to implement is preserved. Conservatism generally rejects Reform's efforts to define Judaism as a creed or a religious sect, stressing rather the unity of the Jewish people and the totality of the Jewish way of life. Educationally the Conservatives continue to emphasize Hebrew for its value in attaining a Jewish identity and in opening the door to Jewish literature and the Law. Modern Hebrew has also been utilized to a considerable extent primarily for its value in understanding the Torah and prayer book used in the present-day synagogue. Conservatives have established a few day-schools but their major efforts have been

---

[13] Eugene B. Borowitz, "Tension in Reform Judaism," *The Christian Century*, LXXXI (June 3, 1964), 729–732.

focused on strong weekday afternoon schools supplemented with Sunday schools.

The fourth ideological subdivision, Reconstructionism, is more of a philosophy than a denomination. Although there is a *Reconstructionist* fellowship to which some congregations belong, the movement does not possess the established structural and organizational identity shared by the three preceding groups. Originated by Mordecai M. Kaplan, a teacher in the Conservative Jewish Theological Seminary.

> Reconstructionism identifies Judaism as the *religious* civilization of the Jewish people. The term "religious" refers . . . to a habitual viewing, sensing, and perceiving of reality not as fixed, final, and closed but as forever in formation and transformation. . . . Jewish religion is the Jewish people's consciousness of the promise of existence and its dedication to the tasks of achieving its fuller realization amidst the affairs of men and nature. . . .
>
> By the same token, Judaism is an *educational* civilization. For Judaism's chief concern is the reorganization of human experience so that it may transcend given limitations and yield new aspects of its inherent promise.[14]

Kaplan has insisted that Judaism must rethink or reconstruct its fundamental ideas with a view toward producing a unified Jewish philosophy adapted to life in the United States. Michael Alper has described some goals of this reconstructed educational program. Among them are the understanding and acceptance of the idea of Jewish peoplehood throughout the world, but particularly in Israel; participation in community life of Judaism; respect for other religious faiths; interest in and support for Jewish cultural expressions in art and literature; participation in programs for social improvements; and the reconstruction of the Jewish religion itself.[15] Various persons and congregational schools have been active in producing curriculums to reach these goals.

In summary, while there are obviously sharp ideological differentiations among the three denominations, there is a tendency for all three educational theories to share a common interest in and concern for Jewish knowledge, history, Law, and serious study. The variations occur primarily at the point of intensity, language, and interpretation. These will be explored in some depth in Chap-

---

[14] Meir Ben-Horin, "Redesigning Jewish Education," *The Reconstructionist,* XXIX (December 27, 1963), 6–7.

[15] Michael Alper, *Reconstructing Jewish Education* (New York: The Jewish Reconstructionist Press, 1957), pp. 144–149.

ter VI as a part of the examination of the types of curriculum in use today.

The Roman Catholic
Philosophy of Education

As indicated earlier, the Roman Catholic schools arose in the nineteenth century primarily in protest against the pervading Protestantism which dominated the common schools. But the gradual disappearance of this kind of sectarianism has also been observed, and one might expect a corresponding awakening of Catholic interest in and support for public education. Such has not been the case. Catholic schools not only continue to exist; this century has witnessed an unparalleled effort to increase their number. The reasons for this phenomenon can be found in the Catholic philosophy of education.

Catholics could never be satisfied just because something objectionable (i.e., Protestant emphasis) was eliminated from the public school. Its removal brought an equally unacceptable condition; that is, the completely secular school divorced from all of the traditional forms of theistic commitment which created the institution in the first place. This flies squarely in the face of a Catholic philosophy of life and the important role assigned to education. For a Catholic, religion is the most crucial fact of his existence. This is the starting point from which all else must take its meaning. Nothing can be more important than the transcendent. But the public school, because of the doctrine of separation of church and state and the First Amendment, usually omits religion from its purview. Many thoughtful Catholics actually question whether the omission of religion has in fact rendered the school neutral. They point out quite forcefully the presence of a nontheistic, secular philosophy which does exist legally as a guiding theory for public education and raise this interesting question. Does not the existence of such a philosophy itself constitute an "establishment" of a kind of humanistic religion? Should this not be forbidden by the doctrine of separation, just as theism has been banned? However one may answer these queries, Catholics find in them sufficient reason to reject the public school as their approved institution. Only a school which places religion at the heart of its total purpose and program can be acceptable.

As McCluskey has pointed out,[16] this centrality afforded religion does *not* mean that the Catholic school exists solely or even primarily to "save souls" or teach the catechism. Both are included in the objectives, but the chief goal is the acquisition of "the supreme integrating principle of supernatural wisdom in ordering the knowledge, skills, and attitudes" with which the school deals. Thus, the Catholic school seeks the same kind of intelligent person that the public school seeks. But it places his spiritual destiny at the heart of his education, and such concerns as knowledge, skills, and attitudes are always subordinate to the supernatural claims known through the Church.

The committed Catholic sees in the existence of God the central factor conditioning his own existence. God has purposed for man both a present and a future life. Man's capacity to reason does lead him to some knowledge of truth and goodness, but his inheritance from Adam (as described in St. Paul's use of the Genesis story) has deprived him of the supernatural gift or capacity to participate in the divine life. To redeem man from this evil condition, God gave Jesus Christ as Savior. Through his grace (that is, unmerited gift from God) reconciliation becomes possible. Knowledge of this restoration does not come by reason, however. God has elected to reveal it only by supernatural revelation in the Bible which was committed to the Church's ministry and interpretation. These are the central truths which constitute the religious faith of Catholic education. Thus, in the words of Pius XI's encyclical on *The Christian Education of Youth,* "it is clear that there can be no true education which is not wholly directed to man's last end." And again, the proper goal of Christian education is "to co-operate with divine grace in forming the true and perfect Christian, that is, to form Christ Himself in those regenerated by baptism." This is not to suggest that the Catholic educator has no interest in the temporal or civic concerns. Again in the words of Pius' famous encyclical:

> The true Christian does not renounce the activities of this life, he does not stunt his natural faculties; but he develops and perfects them, by co-ordinating them with the supernatural. He thus ennobles what is merely natural in life and secures for it new strength in the material and temporal order, no less than in the spiritual and eternal.[17]

---

[16] Neil G. McCluskey, *Catholic Viewpoint on Education,* rev. ed. (New York: Doubleday & Company, Inc., 1962), pp. 57–61.

[17] Pope Pius XI, *The Christian Education of Youth,* Official and Complete English text (Washington, D.C.: National Catholic Welfare Conference, 1930), p. 37.

Hence, the Catholic school contains all of the curricular emphases characteristic of the public schools, such as citizenship, democratic ideals, and the like. But all are set within a theistic, supernatural framework for understanding and interpretation.

Since the state has established educational standards and schools to meet them, many persons would conclude that it has the prior right to educate children of all citizens. This the Catholic Church strenuously denies. Such rights belong to parents and are a product of the natural relationship with their children. This view was sustained by the United States Supreme Court in the *Pierce v. Society of Sisters* decision. The Church readily accepts the state's right and obligation to set minimum standards for the educating of its young. As stated in *Pierce,* it is the family's prerogative to determine the manner by which these requirements shall be met. But the family is not self-sufficient. It seldom can provide the educational experience which is needed, and here the divine jurisdiction of the Church prevails. It alone can provide the eternal dimension without which education is deficient and unacceptable. According to McCluskey, "the Catholic Church, therefore, possesses the pre-eminent right in education—pre-eminent precisely because of the primacy of the supernatural order. The Church holds that her right to teach is a power vested in her directly by her Divine Founder Himself."[18] The Church, thus, stands above all social institutions and is not dependent upon the state for its authority to teach. Any parent who accepts the authority of the Church is automatically committed to follow its precepts and regulations in the matter of the education of his children.

There are many who object to this claim as a kind of ecclesiastical imperialism. Catholics quickly respond by pointing to a variety of court evidences which appear supportive. For example, in 1946 Justice Jackson wrote "that in the domain of conscience there is a moral power higher than the State."[19] In making this claim Catholics are placing their faith at the apex of their values, nothing else (including the nation) being higher. Other theists would still object on the grounds that the conscience implied here is individual, not collective. And, while he may not be reflecting any official Catholic position, McCluskey[20] points out that this "right of private judgment" is really a Protestant doctrine which Catholics are bound

---

18 McCluskey, *op. cit.,* p. 72.
19 *Girouard v. United States,* 328 U.S. 61 (1946).
20 McCluskey, *op. cit.,* pp. 68–72.

to reject. One datum of the committed Catholic's belief is his acceptance of the Church's authority on a wide range of public issues, with education included among them. Thus, the individualistic view of the nature of conscience is unacceptable precisely because it contradicts the Catholic doctrine of the Church. Because he accepts the divine origin of the Church, the Catholic is also prepared to accept its priority in the matter of educating his children.

In summary, education for the Catholic must be one. The so-called secular studies must be integrated with the religious studies. The spirit and content of the religious must permeate and inform the secular. The overwhelming Protestant and Jewish reliance upon one or another forms of supplementary education added to the public school is not acceptable to the Catholic. Nothing less than a separate school maintained by the Church for its own goals can measure up to the demands of the Catholic philosophy of education.

CHAPTER V

Protestant Religious Education Practice

Introduction

It is almost presumptuous to label anything as "Protestant," since the word covers such a wide variety of separate entities. The *Yearbook of American Churches for 1965*[1] identified 224 different denominational bodies, each of which was designated as Protestant. Almost 67 million members were reported by these groups, with more than 40 million persons enrolled in Sunday church school. As one might expect, there is considerable educational diversity, but at the same time there are many common practices.

Most denominations maintain national boards of education which are charged with responsibility for developing and promoting all educational policies and programs. Although their staffs vary from a few to scores of persons, these boards study the needs and opportunities for religious education in their churches. They recommend patterns of organization, specific educational institutions and programs, and they usually produce the printed resources which are required. The publishing enterprise itself is a vast undertaking, particularly in the larger denominations where specific curriculum items sometimes have a circulation exceeding a million copies per issue.

Many of the denominations also have established regional boards of education primarily for the promotion of the program of education which has been chosen by the national board or the denomination itself. Under various titles—synod, presbytery, conference, district, state—these boards direct the services of staff members to the individual local churches within their specific geographical territories. They also often sponsor area-wide programs of their own as additions to the work of the churches. Typical of these nonlocal efforts would be summer camping, youth-work rallies and meetings, Christian higher education programs, and others.

But all of the work at the national and regional level is supplementary and supportive in nature. The heart of Protestantism's educational endeavor always has been and will continue to be in the

---

[1] Benson Y. Landis (ed.) (New York: Office of Publication and Distribution, National Council of the Churches of Christ in the U.S.A., 1965), pp. 252, 260.

local church itself. Each congregation usually has an elected committee, board, or commission on education related to the governing body (session, official board) of the church. This group identifies the educational needs of the local church and plans for meeting them. In its planning it will ordinarily choose to implement those recommended programs from the national board which appear to be most useful. To this end it selects leadership, provides training experiences, purchases curriculum materials, supplies, and equipment, and in general supervises the entire educational undertaking. During the nineteenth century this was ordinarily confined to the Sunday school, but for the past three-quarters century youth work, vacation school, weekday programs, and other non-Sunday morning enterprises have been added to the local board's supervisory duties.

Protestantism has traditionally held that preaching and teaching are inseparable aspects of the life of the Church. Thus, the local church has always striven diligently to hold services of public worship at which the Word of God could be proclaimed and to sponsor educational programs for carrying on the teaching ministry. Often the former has been the primary province of the ordained clergyman, and the latter has been both inspired and guided by laymen. But the teaching office of the minister is a well-established aspect of the Reformation heritage, and effective ministers have always been good educators as well. The preaching function itself must be complemented by the minister becoming the "teacher of teachers," the one professional who assists them in understanding, preparing for, and achieving the church's educational mission. Most authorities agree that the quality of a church's religious nurture program will be directly related to the minister's fulfillment of his educational responsibilities.

Early in this century it became apparent that an educational specialist would be a valuable addition to the professional staff of larger local churches, and the office of director of religious education was established. Graduate programs were quickly instituted in major universities and seminaries for the training of these persons, and the numbers actually employed rose rapidly in the 1920's. The depression years of the 1930's brought a temporary reduction, but the quantity has again increased since World War II to reach the point of more than 10,000 in the 1960's. Under the leadership of the National Council of Churches standards for certification have been established by the denominations, and these usually in-

clude the holding of a master's degree in religious education. In
the local church the director performs essentially those duties
within the teaching ministry formerly assigned to the pastor, but
on a full-time basis. Often his function will include the interpretation of the church's educational task to the entire congregation,
as well as the board of education, and the administration and
supervision of the total program, as well as the actual teaching of
teachers and others within the church.[2] The value and general acceptance of the director of religious education is now universally
established among the major Protestant denominations, and almost
all larger churches either have or expect to employ such a person.

The Church School

The term "church school" is usually used to describe all of the
local church's educational programs, including Sunday school,
weekday instruction, youth work, vacation school, and so on. But
among these programs the most common one is the Sunday church
school. Organized on an age-group basis, it serves children (through
Grade 6), youth (up to eighteen–twenty years of age), and adults.
Very small churches often have only three or four classes for instruction: preschool, elementary school (Grades 1–6), youth, and
adults. Moderate sized congregations refine these divisions somewhat: nursery (through three years of age), kindergarten or begin-
ners (four and five years of age), primary (Grades 1–3), junior
(Grades 4–6), junior high, senior high, and adults. The larger
churches usually establish a "closely graded" school wherein separate departments are maintained for each age through Grade 6 or
even through senior high school in the very largest congregations.
Each local church school is ordinarily administered by a superintendent, often with divisional assistants for children, youth, and
adults. And the separate age-level departments frequently are
headed by a "superintendent," giving the word three different levels
of meaning in administration and supervision.[3]

Almost all church schools are graded—insofar as possible—on
the public school grade basis. Since grading is an effort at the
grouping of pupils for study, this procedure holds the greatest po-

---

[2] Louise McComb, *D.C.E., A Challenging Career in Christian Education* (Richmond: John Knox Press, 1963).

[3] Paul H. Vieth, *The Church School* (Philadelphia: Christian Education Press,
1957), pp. 24–67.

tential for effectiveness. Most churches usually assign students to the church school classes which correspond to their public school grades, regardless of chronological age. Thus far the church has seldom faced the issue posed by public school tendencies toward nongraded instructional groups. If this becomes a widespread practice, adjustments will be forced on Protestant churches. However, rigid adherence to the public school grading pattern has not been accepted without problems. It permits no flexibility for varying degrees of spiritual growth and religious knowledge, nor is it cognizant of other cultural and experiential differences which may be present in an age group. The obviously false assumption has been that all pupils of a given public school class should be taught together. Similarly, it has been only in the 1960's that churches have become aware of the needs of the exceptional child, whether retarded or advanced, and only a few hesitant experiments here and there in the nation are being attempted. Clearly it must be admitted that the question of grading has not been finally resolved in American Protestantism.

As Miller has written, "Christianity begins with love, and love is the first experience of a new-born baby. With all his limitations, the infant's experiences with his parents are the beginnings of religion."[4] Many churches practice infant baptism or dedication as the initiatory rite of participation in the Christian community, and increasingly they are engaging in parental instruction to assist in the religious nurture of the very young. In fact, the parents' class has become a quite common feature of some denominations. Nursery classes for children two and three years of age are their earliest introduction to the church school. Here the quality of relationships will be the chief teaching medium. The kindergarten is for those four and five years old. Activity and group living are the major instructional methods. The elementary grades (1–6) parallel rather closely the types of learning procedures which are found in the public school counterparts, with curriculum materials and activities of comparable difficulty and complexity. They are, of course, focused upon the distinctive objectives characteristic of the churches within Protestantism.[5]

---

[4] Randolph Crump Miller, *Education for Christian Living*, 2nd ed. (Englewood Cliffs, N.J.: Prentice-Hall, Inc., 1963), p. 323.

[5] See Iris V. Cully, *Children in the Church* (Philadelphia: The Westminster Press, 1960); Ethel L. Smither, *Children and the Bible* (Nashville: Abingdon Press, 1960); R. S. Lee, *Your Growing Child and Religion* (New York: The Macmillan Company, 1963).

In its organized relationships with youth the church has generally emphasized three "programs": the Sunday service of worship, the Sunday morning church school, and a Sunday evening youth group meeting. At their best these programs were often independent of each other, and at their worst they became competitive. Since the 1940's a new era in youth ministry has been emerging with the adoption of the "youth fellowship" concept. The emphasis in this approach has stressed a single, united program with youth. The program may have various facets, but all are coordinated by unified planning and administration. At the national level interdenominational coordination has been accomplished by the United Christian Youth Movement, a programming arm of the National Council of Churches. Most churches maintain junior and senior high departments of the Sunday church school, although considerable variety also exists here. In fact, a small minority of these sessions are held on weekdays after public school hours. The evening fellowship meeting is the second customary feature of youth programs. Although not necessarily recommended, the Sunday morning sessions tend to be more formal in their educational structure and are more nearly teacher oriented. The evening programs are generally more flexible and are planned and executed by the youth themselves, with adults playing a much less conspicuous role as counselors. Separate, though integrated, curriculums are made available by the denominational publishers for both types of program.[6]

There is no age-group area of church programming which is filled with more problems than the program for young adults. It is the almost universal experience among the denominations that contemporary young people are not attracted to the church in very large numbers. Our urban centers hold hundreds of thousands of nonchurch-going persons in this 18–25 age range. Yet almost every study of the group has revealed that many of these young people were raised in church families and were active in church youth groups through the high school years. Several of the major denominations have recently given careful attention to this phenomenon, and various experimental strategies are emerging. These unconventional programs are usually operated away from the church buildings, and they have included meetings in coffee houses, chap-

---

6 See Henry A. Tani, *Ventures in Youth Work* (Philadelphia: Christian Education Press, 1957); Oliver DeWolf Cummings, *Youth Fellowship* (Philadelphia: The Judson Press, 1956); and Rowena Ferguson, *The Church's Ministry with Senior Highs* (Nashville: The Graded Press, 1963).

lains assigned to residential areas, and other unusual methods.[7] To date no consensus has become evident from these programs, but the experiments are being continued in numerous cities across the United States.

Other adults who are being served by the church tend to become active in one or another variation of the traditional adult Bible class. The history of these groups goes back to the nineteenth century and the days of the Sunday school's phenomenal popularity. Sometimes organized for couples and at other times for men and women separately, each local church usually has as many groups as the interest of its constituency will maintain. The uniform lessons, details of which are explained below, have been the curricular staple since 1872. Since the lesson scheme is based on the systematic exposition of the Bible, this adult class structure was early known as the "Bible class." In many churches there is considerable emphasis upon group esprit de corps, often called "fellowship." This takes the form of periodic social meetings, and, much less frequently, sometimes includes service projects of various kinds. Currently the typical new class is organized around a nucleus of young couples who maintain their group identity through the years. A new group is organized each five to ten years, or as often as the numbers of persons available permit. Thus, there is little or no "promotion" or movement from group to group, the only changes being at the opposite extremes of age: consolidation of classes for older members when the numbers diminish, and new groups for the newly married couples.

While the great majority of adult programs fall within this description, the quarter century since 1940 has produced much criticism of this pattern. Virtually every evaluative study has demonstrated that the Bible class seems to produce only negligible biblical learning. It is usually teacher-lecture oriented, and the students do little or no studying. Whatever the values which may be derived from the classes, they are seldom commensurate with the stated objectives for the group. Accompanying this criticism has been a recovery of certain theological perspectives regarding the laity.[8] These and a renewed appreciation for the role of service or mission in the life of the Christian have served to provide a new philosophy of Christian adult education. Primary emphasis has been placed on

---

[7] *Older Youth/Young Adult Team Reports* (Nashville: The Methodist Board of Education, 1962).

[8] Howard Grimes, *The Rebirth of the Laity* (Nashville: Abingdon Press, 1962).

small face-to-face groups. Private study, discussion, and service are the techniques used. The groups are usually interest centered, and their tenure is often limited to no more than several weeks or a few months. It is still too early to evaluate these changes, but almost all professional church educators see in them, in one form or another, the future hope of effective adult education within the churches.[9]

Another feature of the church school in the post-war era has been the willingness of congregations to view every weekday as an opportunity for religious nurture. Whereas church buildings were often unused from Sunday to Sunday—except for the midweek prayer meeting and an occasional session of the Board—today they tend to be busy housing various educational ventures. Adult study groups hold breakfast sessions, women's discussion groups meet during public school hours (when mothers are free), and small groups use the buildings for evening meetings. Some churches organize these into formal programs. The Parish Life Conferences of the Protestant Episcopal Church are examples, as are Schools of Christian Living and University of Life formats in other denominations.

Nor is the older adult neglected. Reliance on the Sunday Bible class for retired persons was once the standard pattern. Today most denominations are suggesting and some local churches are sponsoring weekday Golden Age Clubs, as they are sometimes called. These often last for half or even a full day and feature recreation, fellowship, worship, study, hobbies, and other activities of interest for the aged. The upward extension of the life span, as well as the trend toward earlier retirements in business and industry, is providing the churches with ever increasing numbers of active older adults whose most distinguishing characteristic is free time. To date the churches have only begun to become aware of the opportunity implicit in these circumstances, and most of the existing programs remain in the pilot stage.

But the weekdays also belong to children and youth. Almost all denominations recommend additional sessions of the church school, and some churches hold these as two-hour meetings on Sunday,

---

[9] Robert Clemmons, *The Dynamics of Christian Adult Education* (Nashville: Abingdon Press, 1958); David J. Ernsberger, *A Philosophy of Adult Christian Education* (Philadelphia: The Westminster Press, 1959); but for a sharply opposite view see John Fry, *A Hard Look at Adult Christian Education* (Philadelphia: The Westminster Press, 1961).

especially for children ten years old and younger. Others are operating nursery schools during the week for the preschool ages and supplementary after school programs for children of school age. One typical program includes persons from Grade 5 through senior high school. It meets from 4:00 P.M. to 6:45 P.M. weekly, on Wednesday, and each age group participates in an hour's class (using the additional sessions curriculum recommendations), a choir rehearsal, a fellowship supper, and corporate worship. Other congregations, particularly newer suburban churches with limited facilities, have confined the Sunday church school to children in Grade 6 and younger. A Monday afternoon and evening, for example, is devoted to the youth fellowship groups, and a typical three to three and one half hour session will include the equivalent of the Sunday morning class, supper, and the youth fellowship meeting. It must not be inferred that these weekday practices are widespread in Protestantism, for they are not. But, although statistically still small, an increasing number of churches, usually the larger ones, has been turning to the weekday for supplementary programs and time. The trend does appear to be well established, and it will doubtless grow in the years that lie ahead.

The broad outlines of the typical church school programs have been described, but nothing has been said about the persons who operate them. And this is Protestantism's major problem, its leadership needs. For it is axiomatic that no program is ever more effective than those who are its leaders. Traditionally the church school has been a layman's venture. It was invented, organized, administered, and taught by volunteers. Usually their only claim to the positions has been interest, enthusiasm, and willingness to learn. As observed in the section on Jewish education (see Chapter VI), their teachers are usually paid for their services. This enables the synagogues to set certain minimum standards and to expect that they will be met. No comparable "professional teacher" status can be found in Protestantism, although an isolated instance of pay does exist here and there. But its very infrequency proves the generalization. Protestant teachers are volunteers, members of the congregation, who teach from a variety of motives not all of which are harmonious with the educational objectives of the denomination and local church.

Leadership training, as it has been known through the decades, had its formal beginning in the 1860's as an adult education program. Its purpose has always been to provide both preservice and inservice training for the novice and the active teacher. As denominational boards of education were establishing and developing their programs during the latter half of the nineteenth century, the education of church school leadership took a place second only to the production of curriculum materials. Initially these were little more than the publication of various handbooks and guides for individual study and the holding of conventions and institutes for teachers. But as the decades progressed into the 20th century, a variety of programs has emerged and become standardized in most denominations. Working together in the National Council of Churches, the denominations have established the Standard Leadership Education Curriculum which is comprised of a large quantity of courses on Bible, age-group techniques, administration, Christian living, and other topics. Many of the particular facets of the total leadership program take their direction from the standards which have been erected therein.

The major leadership programs now used by local churches would be among the following types. Some churches schedule *leadership classes* for prospective teachers. These may vary from a few sessions to sessions several months in duration, and they range over a broad area, including biblical and theological insights, understanding pupils, orientation to curriculum, some classroom observation, introduction to the materials, and the like. Such classes are often carried on as a part of the Sunday church school program or operated on weekday evenings.

A second training program is the *Workers' Conference* for inservice guidance. Held either monthly or quarterly, such conferences ordinarily include some general topic or discussion of interest and value to teachers of all age groups and departmental meetings. In medium and larger churches the majority of sessions will be by departments only, with the general session held only infrequently. The latter arrangement is doubtless preferred, since it gives a sense of immediacy and relevance to the meetings.

A third type of training experience focuses on *experience under supervision*. Often prospects are recruited to become apprentices. Here they can observe more experienced teachers, have opportunities to discuss the teaching-learning process with the pastor, director, or superintendent, and thus profit from careful supervision in advance of actually assuming the full responsibility for a class. Although on a much restricted scale, the effort here is to capture some of the values in student-teaching programs for public school teachers. All three of these types, as well as the church school *library,* are the work of individual local churches with their teaching personnel.

Groups of local churches—in both denominational and interdenominational combinations—often operate or participate in other leadership experiences. *Laboratory schools* are perhaps the most fruitful training. Here skilled teachers plan and execute teaching units with unskilled teachers being actively involved in the entire process. In this setting learning is not academic. Teaching proposals can be tried experimentally and evaluated almost immediately. The novice teacher receives an experience in effective teaching rather than being told about it. She is active in the planning, observes the plans develop in a normal teaching situation, and has an opportunity to assess the quality of the situation, all under expert supervision. Similar regional programs are *conferences* and *institutes* on Christian teaching. All three of these forms are ordinarily sponsored by the area denominational organization or area councils of churches.[10]

And yet, with all of these efforts at training, no discerning observer is satisfied with the quality of Protestant leadership. Too often none of these experiences prevails. As vacancies occur those who will consent are recruited, given the curriculum materials, and they become fully responsible teachers with no advance preparation. And just as often this error is compounded by the failure to have an active, involved program of inservice training. The teacher is simply left to his own devices and ingenuity except for the minimal amount of supervision received from a departmental or general superintendent. Only a few churches have risen to the level of setting minimum standards of expectation for teachers. And, even in those churches which alone or in cooperation maintain *all* of the enumerated leadership programs, no one is pleased with the result. It is true that there are many devoted and committed teachers in Protestant churches across the country, but few have been adequately trained for the enormous responsibility which the church has placed in their hands.

---

[10] Lee J. Gable, "Selecting and Training the Local Church's Educational Staff," in *Religious Education: A Comprehensive Survey* (ed.) Marvin J. Taylor (Nashville: Abingdon Press, 1960), pp. 275–279; see also Price H. Gwynn, Jr., *Leadership Education in the Local Church* (Philadelphia: The Westminster Press, 1952).

Supplementary Agencies

The most extensive program of religious education operated usually by the regional denominational agencies is the summer camp, conference, or institute. Although the beginnings of these ventures can be traced back into the late nineteenth century, their development was slow until the 1930's. Since the end of World War II, it has accelerated rapidly until today the nation is dotted by camp and conference facilities which frequently operate at capacity during the summer months. And in many places their use continues around the year, particularly on weekends for retreats, institutes, study groups, and other comparable programs. The popularity of both the physical setting and the types of programming has become so great that they are generally considered to be mandatory aspects of a denomination's total religious nurture efforts.

Summer conferences are distinguished from camping chiefly by virtue of their relationship to the facilities. Conferences tend to be focused on some specific training object; i.e., officers of youth groups or adult leaders of youth. Their program can be operated almost any place that affords housing and recreation equipment. In fact, conferences often are held on college campuses or even in urban centers at hotels. In contrast to this the camp pattern makes much greater use of the out-of-doors setting. It has been defined as an "experience of living in the out-of-doors in the Christian community," and the primary stress is upon living together. The conference, on the other hand, emphasizes study. In its use of the surrounding terrain the camp schedule will include nature study, exploratory hikes and trips, campfires, craft activities, work projects, and the like. The goal of camping is an enriching experience with one's peers in a setting of everyday living. Small groups live, study, work, and explore together in an atmosphere which encourages each person to accept his full share of responsibility for the corporate life. Here some actual problems of Christian living will be encountered and can be faced in a normal manner.

Today contemporary camping is taking various forms. Groups of city churches, and even an occasional large church individually, are operating day camps for juniors, age nine to eleven years. City parks, nearby farms, and other sites are usually chosen. Ordinarily these function about six hours, for example, from 9:30 A.M. to 3:30 P.M., requiring only one meal, and including adequate time for transportation to and from the camp. Crafts, recreation, and some study are included. Resident camping with juniors is also very extensive. Usually planned for groups of about 50 or 60, including adult leaders, the denominations are acquiring, developing, and operating ever increasing numbers of camp facilities. Similar programs are arranged for junior and senior high youth, all of which are stressing "real" camping in a rustic environment. It is true, however, that the majority of church-sponsored summer programs with senior high students is still of the conference type rather than camping.

In recent years a new type of camping has been emerging. It does not depend upon a single physical setting for its locus or its program. Travel is the basic focus of the experience. Churches have organized pack trips along the Appalachian Trail, canoe trips on the lakes and rivers of Minnesota, and other similar expeditions. A typical example was recently sponsored by a Methodist conference youth group. Twenty-five persons in five autos (five adults with twenty youth) visited church-agency programs in the eastern United States for three weeks. They stayed overnight in public camp grounds, using small tents and sleeping bags, prepared two meals daily at the campsites, and used the days for travel and visitation. Very careful advance planning of an itinerary which was feasible made this possible. Numerous variations on this pattern are appearing each summer. One denomination conducted a "travel seminar" to Europe in the summer of 1965. Fifty persons (youth and advisors) flew to Paris, rented bicycles, and traveled from place to place visiting museums, cathedrals, and churches. Overnight accommodations were arranged in the vast network of youth hostels which exist in Europe. These are but a few examples of church-sponsored summer "camping" experiences.

A final example of church camping is not age graded in its selection, at least not in the normal manner. It is family camping, or, depending on the type of program, family conferences. Activities are planned for family units—hiking, nature study, fishing, and exploration trips. There are also activities for the women, men, and children in certain age ranges at other times each day. Since about 12 to 15 families constitute as large a group as is practicable, some local church ministers have been encouraging this experience for families within their congregations. Some are arranged for church-owned facilities, and others are located in national parks and other comparable sites. Although only about two decades old, the family camping program has been growing rapidly among churches. Those who have experienced it are convinced that a program of this kind can, over a period of a few years, revolutionize the life of a church. This doubtless helps to account for the increase in numbers of participating churches.

In summary, in the past 25 years particularly, the Protestant church has discovered the out-of-doors and is using it in ever increasing ways. A considerable amount of creative program work has been done, and the churches are finding camping to be a most valuable addition to their building-centered regular endeavors.[11]

Protestant Curriculum Patterns

There seems to be no end to the making of curriculums. Yet, despite their diversity, some broad common features are readily apparent. The totality of experiences within the church and the church school constitutes the actual curriculum, since each such experience obviously does contribute to learning. But the term, as used here, does not denote this breadth. Rather, it is delimited to those materials which have been planned, developed, and printed for use as a major ingredient in the teaching/learning transaction. It is these resources with which we are here concerned in curriculum patterns.

The curricular form with the greatest longevity is the *uniform lesson.* This form dates back to 1872, and, although various alterations have been introduced since then, the basic pattern has remained constant. An interdenominational committee develops a series of outlines for each year. The outlines are built around some biblical theme or topic with a specific scriptural passage identified for exposition and study. They are called uniform because of the use of the same biblical section with all age groups and in all churches. Each denomination separately, or occasionally in cooperation with others, writes its own expositions of the theme and passage, usually publishing them in monthly or quarterly periodicals. The unchanged purpose of the uniform series through the decades has been to provide a plan whereby persons might study the Bible systematically and grow in knowledge of its message with the expectation that the values in the message will be applied to modern

---

[11] Maurice D. Bone, "Camps and Conferences," in *Religious Education: A Comprehensive Survey* (ed.) Taylor, pp. 215–225; see also John and Ruth Ensign, *Camping Together as Christians* (Richmond: John Knox Press, 1958), and LaDonna Bogardus, *Planning the Church Camp* (New York: National Council of Churches of Christ in the U.S.A., 1955).

life's problems.[12] The themes generally alternate between the Old and New Testaments. For example, during 1965 the following appeared: "Matthew—Gospel of the Kingdom" (16 weeks); "A Nation United" (10 weeks); "Growing as Christians" (13 weeks); and "Old Testament Biographies" (13 weeks). The 1966 biblical topics will include: "What Christians Believe" (15 weeks); "The Kingdoms of Israel and Judah" (11 weeks); "Jesus Interprets Old Testament Commandments" (13 weeks); "Spokesmen for God—Isaiah and Jeremiah" (11 weeks); and "Luke—Gospel of Compassion" (2 weeks) which will extend into 1967 for 13 additional weeks. These themes are arranged on a six-year cycle during which the major areas of biblical study are covered. Although many educators are dissatisfied with this curricular pattern, it continues to be the most widely used curriculum with adults. And some denominations are still using it for youth and a few with children.

The uniform lesson plan had hardly been adopted when opposition and agitation for age-graded substitutes arose. But the change in this curriculum came about only slowly. In 1908 a series of graded lessons was approved and a parallel interdenominational subcommittee on graded curriculum established. Two types of materials have resulted from its outlines. One is the *closely graded lessons.* These are primarily for larger local churches "which desire a program of Christian education correlated to the experience and religious needs of its children and youth, and paralleling their year-by-year growth and development."[13] Separate sets of curriculum materials are published for each age group, and churches maintain individual departments for each preschool age group and for each grade in the public school. Promotion occurs year by year from group to group much as in the schools.

But the closely graded materials can be used only in the larger churches, and there are relatively few of these. In 1965 the average Protestant congregation had only 228 members and a church school enrollment of 147 persons. For these and smaller churches the *cycle graded lesson* has been the answer. A departmental scheme of grading is used, usually on a three-year cycle, but occasionally on a two-year basis. For example, the primary department is com-

12 J. Blaine Fister, "Pooling Our Efforts in Building a More Adequate Curriculum of Christian Education for Adults," in *Wider Horizons in Christian Adult Education* (ed.) Lawrence C. Little (Pittsburgh: University of Pittsburgh Press, 1962), pp. 218–221.

13 *A Guide for Curriculum in Christian Education* (New York: The National Council of Churches, 1955), p. 125.

prised of Grade 1 through Grade 3. Its curriculum is three years in length, graded at the second-grade level of needs and ability. Thus, all three ages can be grouped in the same department, or even the same class if necessary. As local churches increase in average size, the trend is toward the two-year format, although its incidence is still in the minority.

The publication of graded materials parallels the uniform lesson process. Outlines are produced cooperatively among the denominations under the coordination of the National Council of Churches. These include themes, scripture passages, and verses for memorization or other special emphasis. From this point each denomination is free to develop its own graded curriculum, often altering or even abandoning the suggested pattern. In its final form the publication is a thoroughly denominational product.

Despite their long continued existence, no one has been thoroughly content with the uniform and graded lesson patterns. This unrest was earlier demonstrated by the *International Curriculum Guide* project of the 1920's and early 1930's. It has resulted in even newer efforts toward self-analysis and improvement. In the 1950's the National Council's Steering Committee for Curriculum Studies asked, "What kind of curriculum is needed by our churches in the task of Christian education?" Seeking answers, a series of study sessions were held between 1957 and 1960. Exploratory curricular foundations in theology, psychology, philosophy, purpose, learning theory, and others were investigated, and the results have been published by Wyckoff.[14] One outcome of the study was the establishment of the Cooperative Curriculum Project by the National Council. Initially 12 denominations agreed to participate, with the number rising to 16. The partners in this enterprise set for themselves some far-reaching goals. Among them are agreement on a new curriculum design, a definition of its scope, the development of guides to areas of curriculum, specific themes or topics for inclusion, the identification of sequences of experience across the life span, and the description of units for teaching-learning experiences. To date there has been little authoritative or final publication of conclusions reached, despite the fact that the schedule of work projected completion by early 1964. It is evident, as shall be noted below, that some individual denominations have profited greatly from this Project, and at least one denominational curriculum has

---

[14] D. Campbell Wyckoff, *Theory and Design of Christian Education Curriculum* (Philadelphia: The Westminster Press, 1961).

been extensively inspired by its philosophy and theoretical framework.

There is one curriculum area in which interdenominational publication takes place. Unlike the uniform and graded lesson series where only outlines are produced, the Cooperative Publication Association is a joint venture among the denominational publishing houses for the publication of weekday, vacation, leadership, camp, and young adult materials. The weekday series is typical of this work. Based upon studies about the Church, the Bible, the world, and Christian living, the Association has produced two-year graded textbooks for use in ecumenical and local-church weekday schools. A similiar young adult project has resulted in about two dozen paperback study books in the *Faith for Life* series. In each instance one of the denominational publishers, acting for all of the others, accepts responsibility for producing a particular curriculum item, the outline for which has been previously determined jointly.

Not all curriculums fall within the scope of the previously described interdenominational series. The past two decades have witnessed several widely used and quite significant denominational departures from the uniform or graded outlines issued through the auspices of the National Council of Churches. The first to appear was produced by the Presbyterian Church in the U.S.A. (now the United Presbyterian Church in the U.S.A.) in the 1940's. Using three annual themes, God, the Bible, and the Church, the *Christian Faith and Life: A Program for Church and Home* curriculum is arranged on a three-year graded cycle. Its major emphasis upon the church's partnership with the home in religious nurture is a distinguishing characteristic, as is its concern for theological integrity. The second major denomination to issue its own totally new curriculum was the Protestant Episcopal Church. The *Seabury Series* was first used in 1955, and in subsequent years additional portions of the total project have been published as well as revisions of the earlier portions. Rejecting the notion that subject matter, whether theological or biblical, should be the central element in the curriculum, this series focused its attention on the learner's current religious experiences. These were called "religious issues," the "situation which comes into being when God acts and man responds or fails to respond."[15] Illustrations of these issues include appreciation for life (Grade 2), right and wrong (Grade 4), freedom and authority

---

15 David R. Hunter, "The Seabury Series After Six Years," *Religious Education*, LVI (July–August, 1961), 249.

(Grade 7), and decision making (Grade 8). The most radical departure in the *Seabury Series* was the abandonment of the traditional week-by-week lesson plan for teachers. Units were envisaged as a year's work, and the teacher was expected to make her own plans for individual sessions. Revisions have modified this practice somewhat with smaller units (although still not on a weekly basis) being made available. Seabury has also pioneered in integrating family worship and group learning processes into its total curriculum.

Other denominations have been engaged in equally far-reaching change. The United Church of Christ, acting through its two former segments (Congregational-Christian and Evangelical and Reformed) issued its new curriculum in 1960. Guided considerably by the United Presbyterian experiences, it shows both marked similarities and significant differences from *Christian Faith and Life*. The Presbyterian Church in the United States (Southern Presbyterian) began its study in 1955, and the 1963 appearance of the *Covenant Life Curriculum* is the result. The 1963–64 year was devoted to an adult-study program providing orientation for the new curriculum, with the full curriculum for all age groups started in 1964. *Covenant Life* seeks to focus Christian nurture within the total life of the church (rather than as a church school adjunct to congregational life), to emphasize adult education, and to recognize that the Christian home and church are inseparably a part of the total educational process. A totally new children's curriculum for The Methodist Church also appeared in 1964. *Christian Studies for Methodist Children* is cycle graded and published in two forms on both a two-year and three-year graded basis. The very extensive influence of the Cooperative Curriculum Project deliberations is immediately evident in this curriculum.

This list of denominations is by no means complete. Rather it is merely illustrative. The years since World War II have been a period of considerable ferment. Almost every denomination has been engaged in curriculum study and innovation, as these few clearly demonstrate.

Protestant Full-Time Weekday Schools

Not all Protestant denominations are satisfied with the foregoing educational programs. Some are unwilling to accept an education which is comprised of the secular public school supplemented by

Sunday, weekday, and summer programs under church auspices. And, just as Roman Catholics and some Jews, they have turned to the full-time day school as the only acceptable alternative.

Protestant proponents of these Christian day schools often criticize the public school in language which is very similar to that used by Catholics. McCluskey's objection[16] to the secular, nontheistic public school is paralleled by Protestants. Rian has written that "the most prevalent philosophy underlying modern American education is that of experimentalism. . . . Experimentalism not only challenges dogma and external authority, but also claims that these can never exist."[17] Thus, while the vast majority of Protestants question this judgment, a small minority maintains that the aims of public and Christian education are incompatible. It is this group which has established and continues to support the Christian day school. They see in this decision their only opportunity for a unified philosophy of education, one in which the Christian faith permeates and informs all of the educational institutions which guide a child—the home, church, and school. To surrender the child to a public school which is neutral or even hostile to this Christian faith is an unthinkable choice. It would involve an admission that education can be dualistic, one part secular the other sacred or religious. The day school exponents insist that the whole child is being educated and that the Christian faith must affect each aspect of his being and his learning. Education which is adequate, i.e., Christian, demands a Christian perspective in the whole curriculum, a Christian world-life philosophy which stands over all and in judgment of all knowledge and understanding. Since the American public school must by law avoid this position, this group of Protestants has turned to the day school.

Various types of Christian schools have been established. Some are *parochial* Protestant schools operated by individual parishes, just as in the Roman Catholic Church. A collection of parishes in an urban center often sponsors *central high schools*, again comparable to Catholic diocesan secondary schools. There are also *private* schools, usually but not always secondary, maintained by an individual or a group of private persons who share a common theological and educational viewpoint. Still another type is the *parent-society* school controlled by the parents of students enrolled. There is often

---

[16] See Chapters IV and VII.
[17] Edwin H. Rian, *Christianity and American Education* (San Antonio, Texas: Naylor Company, 1949), p. 71.

strong local church and denominational relationship in this latter type, but no actual church control exists. This is reserved for the parents themselves who together are an autonomous organization.

Numerous denominations are engaged in the active support of the Christian day school. Lutherans, particularly the Missouri Synod, have maintained an extensive system of elementary and secondary schools for many years. Seventh-Day Adventists have a similar program of control and support. Members of the Christian Reformed Church favor the parent-society type of school, and their institutions collectively are banded together for cooperative enterprises within the National Union of Christian Schools. The National Association of Christian Schools, an affiliate of the National Association of Evangelicals, is a collection of independent and denominational schools with a shared conservative orientation. Several different denominations are represented in the N.A.C.S. membership. Other churches could be listed, i.e., Baptist, Lutheran, Quaker, Mennonite, but these are sufficient to indicate that the movement is an extensive one, not confined to just one or two denominations.

Attendance at the schools is similarly extensive. Since they are so diverse, statistics are difficult to acquire. But a 1963–64 compilation is illustrative. In that academic year 2725 schools were enrolling 333,921 pupils and employing 16,215 teachers.[18] It is obvious that most of the schools are small by public school standards of size. They average about 122 pupils each, but the numbers are on the increase.

And what of their future? No one can predict with certainty. Rising costs and the unavailability of teachers may be as deterring a factor for Protestants as it is for Catholics. But on the other hand, the recent United States Supreme Court decisions in the prayer and Bible reading cases have caused even greater numbers of parents to become disaffected with the public school. And it may well be that their concern will be so great that the Christian day school will appeal to even greater numbers.

In Conclusion

The most compelling question facing Protestantism in the 1960's is the nature of its future educational strategy. For more than a cen-

---

[18] Mark Fakkema, "The Christian Day School Movement," in *An Introduction to Evangelical Christian Education* (ed.) J. Edward Hakes (Chicago: Moody Press, 1964), pp. 376–377.

tury Protestant Christians have been forced to watch the change of their educational institutions. As Lynn has so well described it, the church once was able to depend upon the Sunday school, the public school, and the home as a three-fold collection of integrated, supportive educational experiences. The achievement of its goals in Christian nurture was dependent upon all three. But through the years the character of the latter two has so changed as to make this philosophy unworkable.[19] Chapters I and II have described the manner by which the religious content of the public school curriculum has gradually been eliminated, culminating in the 1962 and 1963 Court decisions. And the experience of the United Presbyterian and Protestant Episcopal Churches has not given much credence to the idea that the church can rely upon the Christian home as a major factor in reaching its goals. This has left the Protestant church to rely solely upon its Sunday church school, in addition to any weekday or summertime supplements which might be added.

But, is this sufficient? It remains the unanswered question, and, unfortunately, in some circles an unasked question. Many Protestants have not even considered their future strategy. They simply assume that the Sunday church school, plus supplements, will be the only educational program available to them. Others are less easy to satisfy, and more penetrating questions are being raised. For example, study groups in some denominations are asking if lay, volunteer church school programs can ever adequately accomplish the tasks in nurture which the churches have set for themselves. Evaluative procedures are indicating the nature of the outcomes now being reached, and they usually fall far short of goals. In the light of these considerations some individuals and churches are beginning to formulate suggestions for changes in strategy, for new institutions, or for radically altered ones.

Earlier chapters have already noted the potentialities being explored in dual enrollment and the teaching about religion in the public school curriculum. Pilot projects already abound in both proposals, and public school personnel are inviting conversation and planning.

A third kind of change in strategy has also been proposed, and this is confined to the program within the church itself. It does not envisage any cooperative program with the school or other external

---

[19] Robert W. Lynn, "Family-Sunday School Partnership: A Chapter in the History of Protestant Educational Strategy," unpublished doctoral dissertation, Union Theological Seminary, New York, 1962.

institution. This strategy takes numerous forms, only one of which can be explored here. But all forms call for the abandonment of the existing church school with its volunteer and largely untrained teachers.

The most extensive idea projected thus far has come from Fallaw.[20] He suggests that the time has come for Protestantism to recapture the teaching office in the ministry. Once an equal emphasis with preaching, Fallaw argues that clergy have ceased to be teachers by and large. If they teach at all it is to instruct those who will teach others, i.e., in a leadership education program. Fallaw proposes no change in the present nursery, kindergarten, and primary departments with their lay teachers. But beginning with Grade 4, he suggests that the minister use after-school hours, Saturdays, and Sundays for teaching older children, youth, and adults. By judicious scheduling one man could teach 100–125 pupils per week in classes of 15–25 each. Fallaw projects a need for one pastor-teacher for every 50–100 family units within a congregation. And, since fewer classrooms and much less expenditure for facilities would be required, these larger staffs could be financed from the savings in building costs.

This is obviously a radical proposal, one that is not likely to be widely adopted. It would entail sharply altered redefinitions of pastoral duties, but Fallaw believes these to be possible. One section of his book deals with the current tasks of ministers which could be performed as efficiently by laymen who would be released from teaching responsibilities and thus made available for reassignment. But the feasibility of this particular proposal is not the point. The fact of the proposal is the issue at question. Is the volunteer taught church school capable of meeting Protestantism's educational needs? If not, what then should be Protestantism's strategy in the future?

These are the questions for the 1960's. They can no longer be ignored. The easygoing presumption that all that is needed is an improved church school is no longer sufficient. The evidence of its inadequacies is too persuasive to ignore. Protestantism is just beginning and must continue to face these questions and devise educational means which are adequate for the challenge of our day.

---

[20] Wesner Fallaw, *Church Education for Tomorrow* (Philadelphia: The Westminster Press, 1960).

CHAPTER VI

Jewish Religious Education Practice

Introduction

Each of the educational patterns explored in this volume owes much to its past, and Jewish education is no exception. Throughout medieval and early modern times in Europe Jews had lived in almost complete social and cultural isolation from the dominant Christian community, and their educational approaches could be unique and internally oriented. Emancipation from this segregation began in Europe at about 1800, and the closely-knit community life of Jewry could never be the same again. In the United States Jews never suffered quite the same intolerance, and their release from colonial and early national strictures coincided almost exactly with the emergence of the Common School Movement. Eager for acceptance in the general community, the Jew quickly and enthusiastically sent his children to these public schools. And thereby he made for himself a major educational problem.

In the ghetto all education was religious. It centered on the sacred Scriptures, the Talmud and other rabbinic sources, their native language, and the Jewish way of life. But the public school pre-empted the majority of the child's time and left available only after-school and weekend hours for religious education. And Jews found themselves torn between their newly won freedoms and loyalty to the larger community, on the one hand, and their faithfulness to their God and their heritage of sacred studies on the other. The commitment to the public school continued, but all the time there was an ever-present fear that supplementary religious education might be insufficient for the tremendous tasks which were entrusted to it.

This problem took other forms also. Supplementary schools could provide only part-time occupations for teachers, and the schools have had to face the dilemma of securing trained instructors who cannot be guaranteed full employment. Further, they have had to compress their religious studies into fewer hours, inevitably eliminating or reducing some elements which in earlier centuries were deemed essential.

According to Pilch, the past 35 years have been particularly prob-
lematical. As the whole of American society has changed, so also
has the Jewish community. The former Yiddish-speaking communities in urban centers are disintegrating, with Jews distributed
much more generally throughout cities. The sense of Jewish community life has radically diminished also. The great majority of Jewish families are native born Americans today, and bilingualism
(English and Hebrew) is found only infrequently. Other cultural
mores tend to be American rather than Jewish. But most important
of all has been the rise of the modern Jewish congregation—Orthodox, Conservative, and Reform. It is very similar to its Protestant
counterpart. It is not a geographical community. Rather, it is a
group of people who choose to join together with each other for
certain chiefly, though not exclusively, religious purposes. And
much of Jewish education has been taken over completely by the
individual congregations, a relatively new phenomena in American
Judaism.[1]

A final aspect of this situation concerns the home. It is a truism
to call the home an educational institution. This is everywhere true,
but it has been peculiarly true of Jewish homes. From the very earliest times (see Genesis 18:19; Exodus 12:26-27; Leviticus 23:43)
the home was consciously used in this manner. Dietary laws were
learned from the management of the household, and the family religious rituals were educative in nature. Through the centuries this
has been a distinguishing characteristic of the Jewish family. It
could not be true to its own identity and mission and fail at these
tasks. But the changes noted above have affected the home as well
as other phases of Judaism, and the effects have been so extensive
that a recent American Association study has concluded that the
home is of little positive value.

> It has become increasingly apparent that a great percentage of the
> student body comes from homes removed from Jewish tradition and
> devoid of Jewish cultural values; the religious and cultural ideas in-
> culcated in the school are not in vogue at home or in the environ-
> ment.[2]

This condition places a tremendous burden on the other educational
institutions. And it may well be an impossible burden, if there are

---

[1] Judah Pilch, "Changing Patterns in Jewish Education," *Jewish Social Studies,*
XXI (April, 1959), 91–98.

[2] Bernard Klein and Judah Pilch, *New Developments in Jewish School Curricula*
(New York: American Association for Jewish Education, n.d.), I, 1.

learnings which can be taught only in this environment. The future alone can determine the seriousness of this challenge.

In summary, these are the circumstances in which Jewish education operates. Informed observers doubt whether there is such a thing as a Jewish community any longer—a social, cultural, and religious entity which has positive educative import. If the child does not in fact live in this kind of environment, then the task of the school is an even greater one. If the child is to have any distinctly Jewish experiences at all, he must have them within the school.

Types of Jewish Schools

The earliest forms of American Jewish education were borrowed directly from Europe. Elementary education was conducted privately in a *heder* school, usually one room of the teacher's home. Here children were introduced to Hebrew and began to read the Pentateuch. A typical community would normally have several *hedarim* offering instruction at graded levels, and a child could move from one to another of these institutions as he progressed in his religious education. While the heder was brought to America and established here, it never achieved a status comparable to that enjoyed in Europe. And during the present century its role has steadily diminished to virtual extinction.

The *Talmud Torah* was the other imported educational institution. In Europe it had provided an intensive study of the Law and its interpretations, and it was this value which the American Talmud Torah sought to preserve. But, since the public school had been accepted, the Talmud Torah was forced to operate as a supplementary institution. Its pupils were expected to attend five two-hour sessions weekly (Monday through Thursday afternoons and Sunday). Control was vested in the boards or committees that established and maintained the schools on a community level or basis. Organizationally the Talmud Torah was almost always separated from the synagogue. Interest in schools of this type reached its peak by the 1920's when many new buildings were erected and considerable attention was devoted to curriculum, financing, and control.[3]

The rise of modern Jewish congregations has already been noted

---

[3] Simon Greenberg, "Jewish Educational Institutions," in *The Jews: Their History, Culture, and Religion* (ed.) Louis Finkelstein (New York: Harper & Row, Publishers, 1949), II, 924–930.

above, and the education of their children quickly came within the purview of the congregation. This was not, however, a totally new condition. The earliest Jewish school in America had been organized in 1731 by Congregation Shearith Israel of New York City. Others followed in the eighteenth and early nineteenth centuries. But, in as much as their programs were held on weekdays, most of these congregational schools ended abruptly with the adoption of public school attendance by Jewish parents. And, taking a cue from Protestantism, Jewish congregations rather quickly confined their teaching to Sunday morning. The communally organized and sponsored Talmud Torah of the late nineteenth and early twentieth centuries was in one sense a protest against the inadequacy of these congregational one-day-a-week institutions which had existed for several decades. And, for a time, the basic impetus for Jewish education shifted from the congregation to the community. But this momentum was not to last, and by the mid-1920's it had largely run its course. As Jewish families moved into newer urban neighborhoods, their communal life was centered in the synagogue or temple. And the control of education once again returned to the agency which had sponsored it in the earliest years of American Jewry. Every congregation desired to have a Jewish school. And the Talmud Torah was gradually diminished in importance. It has been estimated that by 1958 the Talmud Torah was then serving only 13 per cent of the Jewish school population.

Congregational schools usually take two forms. The more intensive utilize the weekday afternoons as well as Sunday, while their counterparts confine their programs to Sunday mornings. The *Sunday Schools* usually offer from 1½ to 2½ hours of instruction weekly for 32 to 35 weeks annually. They are most often associated with Reform Judaism, although recent tendencies have altered this idea somewhat. During the past 15 years numerous Reform congregations have added weekday afternoon schools for two or three additional sessions. And, conversely, numerous Orthodox and Conservative groups, while insisting that the Sunday school is inadequate, hold such schools for the children who either cannot or will not attend the more intensive sessions. Despite the general dissatisfaction with the Sunday school, it continues to be the most popular institution. The latest statistics reveal that about 45 per cent of children enrolled in any Jewish educational program are registered in Sunday schools.

The other congregational form of education is the *Weekday*

School. Designed to provide more intensive religious instruction, these weekday afternoon schools hold from one to three sessions plus Sunday, each session lasting from 1½ to 2 hours. Thus, it is possible for a child to receive between three or four and eight hours of religious education weekly. In a very few instances the older four-day Talmud Torah program is maintained under congregational auspices with Sunday school added. Ordinarily the Hebrew language studies are stressed during the week with primary emphasis being placed on understanding the liturgy and the reading of the Pentateuch. The Sunday schools are reserved for the subjects which may be taught in English and are independent of Hebrew instruction.

Conservative Judaism, which maintains the largest percentage of weekday schools, strives for a minimum of six hours weekly in its schools. Recommended are Foundation, Nursery and Kindergarten, or Primary Schools for children up to seven years of age; Elementary departments for ages eight through eleven; and Junior and Senior High School departments for youth.[4] Since the synagogue is the focus of worship for the families affiliated, the synagogue school is able to relate religious nurture to the home in a direct manner.

Congregational sponsorship of religious schools is not an unmixed blessing, however. The National Study of Jewish Education conducted in the 1950's found numerous congregational schools which were markedly inadequate. Often congregational pride required that a school be maintained even when interest and support were lacking, and the competitive spirit among adjacent congregations actually produced more schools than were needed. The National Study recommended that a communal system of intercongregational support and control be organized that would eliminate the existing divisiveness and instability.[5] Unfortunately denominational and institutional loyalties tend to play a determinative role in these matters. All too often the philosophies of the particular denomination (Orthodox, Reform, Conservative) are taught rather than loyalty to the Jewish people and religion. And this constitutes fealty to only a segment of Judaism rather than to its totality. The operation of schools by individual congregations and denominational

---

[4] *Objectives and Standards for the Congregational School* (New York: United Synagogue Commission on Jewish Education, 1958), pp. 15–19.

[5] Alexander M. Dushkin and Uriah Z. Engelman, *Jewish Education in the United States* (New York: The American Association for Jewish Education, 1959), I, 252.

groups has tended to produce these less desirable characteristics in some instances.

The most intensive form of education within Judaism is the Jewish *Day School*. Surprisingly enough its period of phenomenal growth has coincided exactly with the diminution of the Talmud Torah and the expansion of the congregational schools. Day Schools numbered only 16 in 1935. By 1956 they had grown to 200 and in the fall of 1963 the doors of no less than 293 were opened for full-time religious and secular education! This growth is generally attributed to their promise of providing children with a thorough Jewish religious education, something which a not inconsiderable minority of Jewish parents have not found in the congregational schools whatever their intensity may be.

The Day School provides the *total* education for the child, religious as well as secular. As such attendance constitutes a substitute for the public school, the curriculum reflects this combination of motivations. About half of each day is spent in religious (commonly called "Hebrew") studies which emphasize the Bible, the Hebrew language, the Talmud, and the Code of Jewish Law. Primary stress is placed on observance; that is, gaining an understanding of and commitment to the Jewish way of life. The balance of the day is devoted to "English" studies which comprise the curriculum required by state law. Thus there is a blending of general and religious education with a distinct effort being made to correlate the two into a philosophy of life.

Most Day Schools attempt to be communal in form, with lay and rabbinical leadership drawn from the community. But, while it is true that they receive students from the various denominational ideologies, Orthodoxy is clearly dominant. Precisely because the Orthodox claim the great concern for the Torah and Hebrew language, they tend to be the element within the Jewish community which is most interested in intensive Jewish education. Hence, it should not be surprising that more than 90 per cent of Day Schools proclaim a distinctly Orthodox viewpoint. Although children are accepted from all segments of the Jewish community, only the Orthodox philosophy is taught. The remaining 7 or 8 per cent of Day Schools are either Conservative or Zionist in sponsorship.

The major problem which confronts the Day School leadership is probably the financial one. All charge tuition, usually $400–$500 per year, but per capita expenditures exceed this sum considerably. Thus, community financial drives, participation in the Jewish fundraising agencies, and other similar measures are ever-present concerns. And an interesting inconsistency in Jewish thinking occurs at precisely this point. Jews tend to be among the most vocal proponents of separation of church and state, opposed to any breach in this "wall of separation." Yet the devotees of Day Schools are nearly unanimous in their desire to receive federal aid for their schools. And they use virtually the same arguments which the Roman Catholics advance for this request (see Chapter VII).[6]

The Day School is clearly filling a need within Judaism, and its strength is not its similarity with but rather its difference from the other forms of Jewish education. There is a substantial minority of Jewish parents who seek the traditional, intensive Jewish education for their children. Among all of the alternatives available the Day School is the sole one which appears capable of fulfilling the demand.

One of the major inadequacies of Jewish education is at the secondary level. The 1958 national survey revealed that from 40 to 45 per cent of the 5–14 year age group was receiving religious education in that year, but only 14 per cent of the high school age was enrolled. Thus, about two of every three Jewish children who receive elementary education do not continue their studies! One obstacle to high school study is the strong Bar Mitzvah tradition which views this ceremony as "graduation" and attainment of manhood. And yet, just as both Protestants and Catholics have been discovering, these are crucial years for the religious faith of the youth. As one critic has observed, all too often "a youth's abandonment of the Jewish school generally results also in his estrangement from Judaism."[7] It should be noted that high school participation does seem to be on the increase, in comparison with former decades. But this remains a major problem the extent of which is made obvious by the fact that in any given year only one of seven youths of high school age can be expected to be enrolled for religious study in either the synagogue, temple, communal high school, or all-day school.

It should be evident that despite certain gaps in the Jewish

---

[6] Joseph Kaminetsky, "The Jewish Day Schools," *Phi Delta Kappan,* XLV (December, 1963), 141–144; "Evaluating the Program and Effectiveness of the All-Day Jewish School," *Jewish Education,* XXVII (Winter, 1956–1957), 39–49; and *Jewish All-Day Schools in the United States,* Information Bulletin No. 22 (New York: American Association for Jewish Education, 1953).

[7] David Rudavsky, "The Status of the Jewish Secondary School," *Religious Education,* LVI (March–April, 1961), 99.

school's coverage of the school-age population a rather considerable proportion of the group is receiving instruction. The National Study of 1958—the latest data available—concluded that "well over 80 per cent of Jewish children receive some Jewish schooling at *some* time during the eight years of elementary school age."[8] This would seem to support the idea that the overwhelming majority of Jewish parents is interested in education and does endeavor to make the necessary provisions for obtaining it.

The next obvious question concerns the extent of this instruction. While 80 per cent are enrolled at one time or another, this tells us nothing of the length of enrollment. The statistics derived from the National Study are not explicit at this point, but the authors have drawn some conclusions on the basis of sampling. And it is their judgment that the average length of stay is three years for the Weekday School and four years for the Sunday School. Thus, only about half of the six-year curriculum is completed, and it tends to be the earlier portion rather than the later. Enrollment in the first three or four elementary grades tends to be much higher, but the rate of retention decreases with progress through the school. Thus, it seems quite clear that Judaism has a major problem in reaching and retaining its children and youth in the educational programs which are provided.

Curriculum Patterns for Jewish Education

Any attempt to describe Jewish education curricula is immediately presented with a serious dilemma. While there are three national commissions organized around the denominational ideologies, each Jewish school is independent. It may choose to accept and implement all, only a portion, or even none of its commission's program. Thus, it is necessary here to describe the *recommended* curriculums and then turn to the *actual* curriculums revealed by the first National Study of 1958.

Orthodoxy's curriculum is committed to the full mastery of the Torah. Nothing less than this will suffice, since the divine guidance for life which every devout Jew desires can be found there only. Its curriculum is designed to apply the values contained in the Torah to the choices of daily living. To this end the various Mitzvoth (commands), Sabbath observance, Holy Day practices, dietary laws, social justice, and ethical implications are focal points for

---

8 Dushkin and Engelman, *op. cit.,* p. 44.

curriculum construction. The Hebrew language is the language of instruction, as soon as it is learned, and the direct study of the Torah and Talmud is essential. Other subjects within the curriculum are Jewish history, civics, and the State of Israel.[9]

Conservatism's commission has suggested that the curriculum be grouped around three emphases. (1) Torah and Hebrew language: the elementary school should make Hebrew language its primary subject, since it is the historic tongue of the Jewish people and knowledge of it is essential for Torah study. At the junior high school level Bible, selections from the Talmud and other rabbinic sources, and the ethical and moral teachings of Judaism should be central. (2) Jewish Living: the development of the "basic knowledge, skills, habits, and attitudes necessary for ethical living." Included are subjects and units on the synagogue, the holidays and festivals, participation in Jewish community life, prayer, and worship. (3) The Jewish People: an understanding of the Jewish past and present. Specific subjects included are Jewish history, with particular attention to the role that religious faith has played and Judaism's contributions to world civilization; Israel, appreciation for its importance and the development of a desire to assist in its upbuilding; and an understanding of the history and development of the American Jewish community. Conservatism recommends that these curricular emphases be included in a program which operates from nursery school through senior high three days per week.[10]

Reform Judaism's curriculum is designed primarily for the one-day, Sunday school program typical of its congregations. However, there are additional or alternate subjects recommended which may be used in the congregational schools which have added weekday sessions. Reform appears to be moving in the direction of more intensive instruction, and its currently alternative two- or three-session curriculum may well become the basic Reform curriculum of the future. The Primary Department includes kindergarten and Grades 1–3. In addition to worship, its curriculum is confined to study of Bible and Jewish heroes and understanding of the Jewish holidays. Hebrew language instruction begins in Grade 3. The Intermediate Department comprises Grades 4, 5, and 6. Its curriculum includes Hebrew, post-biblical and American Jewish heroes, ethical living,

---

[9] *A Model Program for the Talmud Torah* (New York: The Union of Orthodox Jewish Congregations, 1942), pp. 12–14.

[10] *Objectives and Standards for the Congregational School* (New York: United Synagogue Commission on Jewish Education, 1958), pp. 9–14.

biblical history, and holiday history and practice. It is surprising to observe that Bible study per se is listed as an alternative study rather than a regular part of the curriculum! The Junior High Department continues Hebrew instruction and worship, medieval and modern Jewish history, personal ethical living, the prophets and sacred writings from the Bible, Reform Judaism, and comparative religions. Interestingly enough the American Jewish community and the State of Israel are here listed as alternative rather than central. The High School Department continues language study, and makes provision for Confirmation at Grade 10. Other aspects of the curriculum include History, post-biblical literature (Talmud), modern Jewish problems, Jewish ethics, beliefs (theology), and current events. And the curriculum outline concludes by adding that Reform education must not end here. Every temple must sponsor continuing education in regular adult classes.[11]

Reconstructionism, lacking the denominational identity of the other three groups, has no comparable commission on education or an established curriculum guide. Nonetheless leaders of this philosophy have been active in rethinking educational theory, and various published curricular suggestions are available. Above all Jewish education must reflect the concept of Judaism as a civilization. The curriculum must be designed to produce active participation in the Jewish civilization rather than stress accumulation of knowledge or other subject matter. Schools should be communally operated rather than congregational, although the latter may be units in a larger totality. Until a child is six years old the curriculum will be home centered, the only Jewish atmosphere which a young child knows. This includes living concretely all the phases of Jewishness which are characteristic of the home, such as holiday observance. From ages six to eleven Hebrew language (4–6 hours weekly) and identification with the Jewish people are stressed. The major formal education starts at age eleven and extends through high school. Requiring at least two sessions weekly, it will stress the history of the Jewish people, their present status, the nature of the Jewish religion, and the Jewish way of life. The goal is to portray Judaism as an on-going civilization with a future as well as a past. The good Jew is certainly loyal to the past, but he has the obligation to correct and improve the heritage.[12]

---

[11] *An Outline of the Curriculum for the Jewish Religious School* (New York: The Union of American Hebrew Congregations, n.d.), pp. 27–34, 75–76.

[12] "Reconstructionism and Jewish Education," *The Reconstructionist*, XXIX (October 18, 1963), 17–22; and XXIX (November 1, 1963), 16–21.

Meir Ben-Horin has proposed that the reconstructed Jewish education be built around answering these questions:

(1) What kind of person am I? How did I come to be what I am? Where and how shall I go from here?
(2) What kind of people do I belong to? How did they come to be what they are? Where and how do we as a people know where to go?
(3) What kind of world is it in which we live? How may we understand its being and becoming.[13]

To this end the Ben-Torah (Son of the Law) plan has been proposed. It shifts the focus of education to the 17–21 age group. Its curriculum stresses sociological analysis and the understanding of current affairs, the history of Judaism, the literary-cultural heritage, and Jewish religion. Specific courses and textbooks have even been suggested. This obviously involves a radical restructuring of current Jewish educational thinking. At the present the great majority of Jewish children terminate their education at Bar Mitzvah, and many cease attending even earlier. Reconstructionism is insisting that the crucial years for Jewish education are those junior and senior high school years which are seldom used for any Jewish education in the contemporary practice.[14]

So much for theories of curriculum as proposed by the educational authorities. What is the curriculum actually found in the Jewish schools? In one sense a proposed curriculum may be judged to be no more effective than its implementation achieves, and the 1958 National Study provides some significant data for judgment.

For example, note the statistics for the teaching of the Hebrew language. While 88 per cent of the schools sampled do teach Hebrew, the majority offer it for only four years or less. And the average time per week is 1½ hours, 36–38 weeks annually. By comparison this is the equivalent of only 1½ years of public school (five days a week) language study, hardly enough to attain even elementary proficiency. Thus, while Hebrew is described as "the breath of life of Jewish religious culture" and "the link uniting all Jews of all times and all climes," "ideal and reality are far apart." Probably no more than 10–15 per cent of the pupils learn sufficient Hebrew to read even the simplest of Bible texts. Clearly the worthy

---

[13] Meir Ben-Horin, "Redesigning Jewish Education," *The Reconstructionist,* XXIX (December 27, 1963), 7.
[14] Emanuel S. Goldsmith, "The Ben-Torah Plan," *The Reconstructionist,* XXIX (November 1, 1963), 6–12.

goals which are set forth in the official statements of curriculum are far from realized in language instruction.

Unfortunately Bible study is hardly better. The universal hope is that students will read the Bible in the original Hebrew, but few receive sufficient preparation to permit this. Those who are introduced to the Hebrew Torah face the insurmountable barrier of inadequate language understanding. But what of Bible study in English? The record is not much better here. Fully 70 per cent of the Sunday schools were discovered to be teaching no Bible at all, either in Hebrew or in English! And in the Weekday Afternoon Schools, the quantity of instruction proved to be the equivalent of only a one-year literature course. Only in the Day Schools was Bible instruction very extensive. But this can hardly make any sizeable impact on Judaism when it is recalled that only 8 per cent of the students are in these schools.

Similar results were discovered about the teaching of the Talmud. Jewish history, customs, and ceremonies fared somewhat better, perhaps because of the absence of the linguistic barrier. But even here the extent of the study and the degree of mastery were seriously limited by the inadequacy of time available for instruction.

The authors of the National Study conclude: "the likelihood is that the vast majority of our children grow up without *any* knowledge of the Bible text, either in Hebrew or English. . . . Are we to cease being 'the People of the Book'?"[15] Hence, the observer is forced to conclude that Jewish education's worthy goals, as stated in the various curriculum guides and outlines, are frequently ideal. They are hardly being reached at any point, and the reasons are two-fold. Pupils do not attend long enough each week, nor do they continue their religious education for a sufficient number of years to permit excellence. The curriculum is distinguished. Its execution in individual religious schools is all too often deficient.

Personnel and Organizations in Jewish Education

Just as in any educational program there can be no serious question raised about the importance of the teacher of religious subjects. He is all important. Even the best of curriculums will be ineffective without proficient instructors. All of the agencies sponsoring Jewish

---

[15] Dushkin and Engelman, *op. cit.*, p. 189.

education recognize that serious problems prevail in respect to teaching staff.

Sunday schools are staffed generally by women who teach two or three hours weekly and are paid from $135 to $400 annually. The teacher's own Jewish education is probably just from her own elementary school years, and it is improbable that she has had any pedagogic training. Only one in five is licensed. Weekday School teachers tend to be men who spend from 8 to 20 hours weekly in the classroom. They earn from $1500 to $4500 per year, and about two-thirds look upon teaching as their main occupation. Sixty per cent of those who are employed full-time are licensed, but 40 per cent of the part-time teachers also hold teaching certificates, and 84 per cent speak Hebrew. Day School instructors have received the most training of all: 92 per cent speak Hebrew; 77 per cent received training in a Jewish teacher training institution; and 95 per cent definitely look upon teaching as their careers. They earn between $3500 and $6000 annually for teaching 15–30 hours per week.[16]

From these data it is obvious that Judaism suffers from a severe shortage of qualified teachers. Only a minority receives compensation adequate for full-time employment and the limited financial rewards make it difficult for school principals and boards to set very high standards. To this inadequate preparation must be added a rapid rate of turnover. The solution appears to lie in a basic shift in Jewish community attitude toward education in general and teaching in particular. Only when Jewish parents are so desirous of quality education that they are willing to pay the high price of excellence can sufficient persons be attracted to teacher training and ultimately to teaching. These potentialities are not immediately apparent in the contemporary Jewish community.

The total local community concern for education is expressed through a *bureau of education*. Although having various titles, some 40 communities now have such an agency. Historically it has been a kind of educational service agency for setting standards, promoting improved teacher training, coordinating youth activities, distributing subsidies from the Jewish federation and community chest, and in general interpreting Jewish education to both Jews and the community at large. A few "intercongregational" schools are sponsored by some local bureaus. At present there is lively interest in

---

16 Dushkin and Engelman, *op. cit.*, pp. 112–124. These financial data are from the Study conducted in the 1950's. They are doubtless higher today, but no comparable statistics are available.

the future role of the bureau. The national agencies, which are considered below, tend to pre-empt on a denominational basis numerous functions previously provided by the bureau. There are numerous tasks which must be performed in unity, and the bureau of education is the only agency which lends itself to this type of task. The provision for teacher training is only one obvious example of such important functions.

Nationally there are two types of agency with major influence on Jewish education. Each of the three denominations maintains its own commission on education. Chapter IV examined the philosophies of education held by these agencies, and the preceding section of this chapter described their proposed curriculums. *The Commission on Jewish Education of the Union of American Hebrew Congregations* is the Reform body. Organized in 1916 the department seeks to clarify aims, provide guidance in curriculum, publish materials, and maintain a program of liaison among the Reform congregations. Conservatism's agency is known as the *Commission on Jewish Education of the United Synagogue of America.* Although relatively new, having been organized in 1949, it holds purposes for its Conservative constituency which are very similar to those of Reform. Orthodoxy's efforts are not quite so unified as the other two denominations. The Day School movement is guided by *Torah Umesorah* (the National Society of Hebrew Day Schools), which was organized in 1944. Since that date it has assisted in the establishment of more than 100 Day Schools and provides a variety of services in curriculum, supervision, publication, and staffing. The *National Council for Torah Education* is a Zionist-oriented agency with more than 140 affiliated Day and Weekday Schools. It assists in organization and supervision of its schools, provides placement and curriculum services, and sponsors the National Commission for Yeshiva Education. The departments of the commission serve as professional societies for principals, teachers, lay leaders, and parents groups in the Day School movement.

The *American Association for Jewish Education* seeks to serve as an all-encompassing body for Jewish education, transcending the ideological and denominational boundaries which otherwise tend to divide. Organized in 1939, the more than 40 local community bureaus throughout the United States are affiliated members. The American Association is committed to the principle of total Jewish community responsibility for education. It seeks to "stimulate, promote, extend and improve the status of Jewish education on all age levels." It offers services in research, community organization, curriculum and instruction, personnel and teacher training to local congregations, bureaus, educational agencies, and organizations.[17]

In Conclusion

There can be no question that interest in Jewish education is on the increase in America. Although the rise in Jewish population during the 1948–58 decade was only about 15 per cent, the growth in Jewish school enrollment was a phenomenal 131.2 per cent! But the meaning of the statistics is not quite as clear as these raw data might seem to imply.

As numerous Jewish critics have commented, there may well be no identifiable entity called "Jewish education." Varieties of practice covered by this blanket title are too wide for much meaning any longer, and they would appear to be growing even greater annually. Much of what is labeled "Jewish education" is so small in scope and brief in duration that it simply begs the question to so label it. If knowledge of the Hebrew language, the Bible, and the Talmud are valid goals for Jewish education, then a considerable portion of so-called Jewish education must be branded as a failure.

The National Study of Jewish Education did seem to indicate that Jewish parents are increasingly interested in religious schools of a high quality. But unfortunately this image of expectation has all too often been projected without an accompanying commitment to providing the conditions necessary for its attainment. The National Study identified these conditions in this manner by stating that parents must:

(1) *arrange for their children to give more time to Jewish study;*
(2) *help them continue in Jewish school beyond the Bar-Mitzvah or Confirmation, during the crucial years of adolescence;*
(3) *insist that their children be taught by full-time, well-trained knowledgeable Jewish teachers; and*
(4) *provide in their homes and in the community an atmosphere of respect and desire for Jewish culture and learning.*[18]

The goals and objectives or philosophy of education sound very much alike to the reader of curriculum guides published by the denominational groups. In fact, to the uninitiated they appear to be virtually identical. Hebrew language, Bible and Talmud study, Jew-

---

[17] Judah Pilch (ed.), *Jewish Education Register and Directory* (New York: American Association for Jewish Education, 1959), II, 47.
[18] Dushkin and Engelman, *op. cit.*, p. 224 (italics in the original).

ish living, and understanding Jewish history and culture appear in each. The real differences among the denominations are not found in stated objectives. Rather they appear in the extent to which each is willing to go to reach these goals. Reform may well espouse an interest in the Hebrew language, but the claim is the very essence of futility in a Sunday school with its typical attendance patterns. A similar claim offered by Orthodoxy is much more meaningful when parents are willing to finance an All-Day School in order to reach their expectation. Congregations collectively and parents individually must decide just how far they are willing to go in order to reach these goals. Of course, money is not the sole factor in determining quality of results. But it does have the potential ability to create conditions in which good results *may* be achieved. When wisely spent for good textbooks and well-trained leaders, its importance is unquestioned. It would appear that to date the Conservative and Orthodox have been more willing than Reform to make available these conditions.

The authors of the National Study point clearly to the obvious inadequacy of the Sunday school. Faced with the tasks accepted, it can hardly claim to be defensible. And they recommend that it be used solely for the five- to seven-year primary department. From age eight and upward the weekday school plus Sunday school would appear to be essential and its program should proceed through the balance of the public school years.

Judaism in America appears interested enough in high quality religious education. Whether it will make the necessary sacrifices in order to achieve it is its dilemma for the future.

CHAPTER VII

Roman Catholic Religious
Education Practice

Introduction

The decade of the 1960's is in many ways a period of intense test-
ing and self-analysis for Roman Catholic educators. Caught in the
press of the population explosion, their schools are beset with economic problems that a quarter century ago could hardly have been
anticipated. And, although Catholic education has always been subject to considerable *external* criticism, the peculiar and intense
demands of contemporary living have raised a not insignificant
number of *internal* critics. Today the academic excellence of the
schools is being questioned from within, as is the policy of emphasis
upon elementary education often at the expense of secondary institutions. All in all, Catholic education has certainly come of age, but
it finds its time of maturity to be a crossroads experience of new
decisions.

The nineteenth century circumstances and forces which produced the Catholic school system have already been outlined, as
was the basic philosophy of education. The 1884 decree of the
Third Plenary Council requiring that each parish establish an elementary school has been the ideal for the Church since that day.
It is sometimes summed up succinctly in these words: "Every Catholic child in a Catholic school." And the purpose and goal has been
equally clear. In the words of Gerard Sloyan, "Roman Catholic
religious education may be defined as *the unfolding of the terms
of God's gift freely given—life—and of the response of free acceptance to that gift.*"[1] This is an unmistakable emphasis upon religious centrality. The schools are one major facet of the Church's
efforts to reach its religious goals, and this fact doubtless contrib-
utes to the popularity of the schools with Catholic families. But it
must not be presumed that this focus upon the Christian religion
is accomplished to the exclusion of other goals. As Brickman has

---

[1] Gerard S. Sloyan, "Roman Catholic Religious Education," in *Religious Education: A Comprehensive Survey* (ed.) Taylor, p. 396.

observed, the Catholic school must conform to the educational expectations of the public school in academic attainments which might be termed secular. The graduate is expected to be equally as knowledgeable as his public school counterpart.[2] Thus, a dual purpose can be observed in the operation of the schools by the Church.

The 1918 *Code of Canon Law* implements this philosophy and the objectives identified by the Baltimore Councils. A brief exploration of certain of its provisions will be useful. Canon 1375 proclaims the responsibility and authority of the Church over education in general and the schools specifically. Canon 1379 charges the bishops with the exercise of this function and extends the range of application from elementary school through the university levels of education. Canon 1381 further delineates the bishop's role to include the religious training of all youth to the extent of approving of schools, teachers, textbooks, and all other factors which are of import in determining the quality of religious instruction which youth receive in the diocese.

Canon 1113 details the Church's theory regarding parental rights in educational choices. It must be understood in relationship to Canon 1375 (noted above) which identified the role of the Church in providing a religiously acceptable means whereby this parental right may be exercised and fulfilled. Canon 1374 is, in a very real sense, the most crucial of all. Herein children of Catholics are required to attend only the school which can supply this form of education, i.e. the institutions of the Church. It concludes by reserving for the bishop alone the right to grant exemptions and exceptions to the rules.

These are the goals of the Church and the laws which have been adopted to implement and enforce them. The next logical inquiry is their application. And it becomes necessary to examine the extent to which local parishes and dioceses have been successful in these matters.

To answer these questions summarily, one must conclude that since World War II it has become increasingly evident that Catholics have not been very successful. The goal of every Catholic child in a Church school has not been reached, and the educational leaders of the Church doubtless feel at times that they are riding something of a treadmill—running very rapidly in order to stand

---

2 William W. Brickman, *Educational Systems in the United States* (New York: The Center for Applied Research in Education, Inc., 1964), p. 61.

still and avoid any falling farther back. Parochial schools are certainly being built in increasing numbers, but the growth in Catholic school-age population also expands just as rapidly. Some of the most recent statistics illustrating the degree of dilemma involved are given below.

In 1964 the *Official Catholic Directory*[3] reported 10,452 parish elementary schools in addition to 450 private (operated by religious orders) elementary schools, or a total of 10,902 schools enrolling 4,556,616 Catholic pupils. In just six years, since 1958, 1249 new schools had been opened (for an increase of 13 per cent), but these (plus enlargements to the existing institutions) are still able to enroll only one-half of the Catholic elementary-age school population. This 50 per cent achievement had also been true in 1958! Such illustrates the treadmill figure noted above.

In secondary education the figures are even less encouraging. Despite the existence in 1964 of 2458 secondary schools (1557 parish or diocesan and 901 private) enrolling 1,068,394 students, this represented only about one-fourth of the Catholic population in this age group. And yet, as early as 1911 the National Catholic Educational Association had urged an upward extension of the elementary school ideal to include all of secondary education. The goal of Catholic education has not been reached. All efforts expended notwithstanding, in 1964 only about one-half of elementary-age school children attended Catholic schools, and about three-fourths of secondary school pupils were denied admission. More than 4⅓ million of these public school enrolled Catholics did receive released-time religious instruction. But, judging from the official philosophy of the Church, such supplemental education is inadequate and actually at variance with the theory of education espoused.

A 1958 survey of diocesan regulations clearly illustrates the discrepancy between goals and achievements.[4] Despite the authority granted to the bishop by canon law, only a few more than half had diocesan regulations requiring Catholic school attendance and a goodly number of these had no regular provision for enforcing the requirement. Only 12 of 104 reporting dioceses indicated the possibility of penalties for failure to observe the regulations, and instances of enforcement were very rare indeed.

---

[3] *Official Catholic Directory* (New York: P. J. Kenedy & Sons, 1964).
[4] Cited by Neil G. McCluskey, *Catholic Viewpoint on Education,* rev. ed. (New York: Doubleday & Company, Inc., 1963), pp. 102–104.

These data certainly must not be interpreted as an indication of difference between official policy and actual goals. Catholics are very much interested in their schools, and the ideal is in fact their goal. Unfortunately it has not proved to be realistic. Population growth and economic considerations have combined to make the ideal unreachable.

Patterns of School Organization

The chief school officer for the diocese is the bishop in whom the authority for the control of education resides, according to canon law. Ordinarily he delegates this responsibility to an assistant known variously as secretary for education or superintendent of schools. All schools within the geographical bounds of a diocese are subject to the bishop's jurisdiction, even those maintained by religious orders. Hence, officially the Catholic schools of a given diocese constitute those which have been authorized and recognized by the bishop.

The 1884 Plenary Council authorized diocesan boards of education to assist in the implementation of its mandatory edict regarding elementary education. Such boards continue to exist today chiefly in an advisory capacity to the bishop and superintendent. The superintendent ordinarily will have a staff of professionally trained priest-educators who supervise various facets of the diocesan program, i.e., subject-matter coordination and so on. The Catholic University of America in Washington, D.C., has played a prominent role in the training of these educators who lead the regional programs across the nation. Professional associations, such as the National Catholic Educational Association, provide insight and inspiration for these and other Catholic educators. The National Catholic Welfare Conference's department of education is similarly active in the support of Catholic education's efforts to raise its standards of achievement.

The typical, well-known Catholic school is a parish (called "parochial") institution. The local pastor is its general overseer, engaging the faculty, operating the budget, guiding maintenance, and all the myriad of other functions essential for keeping the school alive. Ordinarily the actual supervision of the educational program is delegated to the priest/brother/sister who serves as principal, but the pastor continues to be centrally involved in all of the concerns associated with education. Parish schools exist at both the elementary and secondary levels, although the former are by far the more numerous.

Secondary schools operate at both the parish and diocesan level. The trend today appears to be toward large, central high schools maintained by the diocese for elementary school graduates from all of the parish schools. Both the parish and diocesan high schools are usually comprehensive in nature offering both terminal and college preparatory programs. Catholics have not generally adopted the junior high school pattern, preferring the 8–4 division of years. Since the early years of this century Catholics have striven mightily to increase the number of secondary schools available to their youth, but the results have not kept pace with the demand. In 1964, for example, Catholic secondary classrooms served only 1,068,394 pupils while another 1,249,137 were attending public high schools and receiving Catholic religious instruction in weekday released-time classes. To these must be added the unnumbered secondary school-age Catholic students who neither attend parochial school nor participate in any supplemental program for religious education. As noted above, these two categories constitute about three-fourths of the 14–18 age group among Roman Catholics.

Although in one sense all Catholic education is private in that it is not operated by the public nor supported by tax funds, Catholics use the term private to designate a third kind of school in addition to the parish or diocesan categories. These are the institutions operated by religious orders. In 1964 there were 450 elementary and 901 secondary schools of this type enrolling 476,426 pupils, or about 8½ per cent of the total. The secondary schools tend to be college preparatory in purpose, although not exclusively. Since they do not have the financial backing of a particular parish or diocese behind them, all charge tuition which is usually quite expensive, in many instances approximating college tuition. Students include both day and boarding pupils. The considerable cost associated with such schools inevitably tends to confine them chiefly to the sons or daughters of the more affluent. And paradoxically, despite their distinctive Roman Catholic religious instruction, in many places these academies have become desirable status symbols for non-Catholic parents who seek to enroll their youth in them.

Catholic higher education began almost as early as Catholic education for the lower schools, and the interest continues undiminished today. The first institution for men was probably Georgetown, which opened in 1789. Colleges for women opened about a century later, reflecting the delayed emphasis upon higher education for women among all Americans, not just Catholics. Most women's colleges emerged as upward extensions of secondary institutions. The first was probably the College of Notre Dame of Baltimore which started its program in 1895. This pattern of separate institutions for men and women has generally continued to prevail up to the present, although many of the larger urban Catholic universities are coeducational.

Canon 1379 of the *Code of Canon Law* extended the philosophy regarding Catholic education upward to include higher education. This decision was left with the bishop to implement whenever and wherever he determined the existence of a need. By 1964 the initial Georgetown efforts of 1789 had grown to encompass a total of 295 Catholic colleges and universities enrolling 366,172 students, by far the largest involvement in higher education of any religious group. And yet, surprisingly enough, only a handful of Catholic junior colleges are included in this number. This is surprising primarily because the junior college represents the most rapidly expanding type of higher education institution, and each year more than 20 per cent of the new freshmen are enrolled in them. These data simply indicate the extent to which Catholicism's dilemma of inadequate educational capacity plagues the Church's colleges and universities as well as its elementary and secondary schools. McCluskey stated that in 1962 two-thirds of Catholics enrolled in higher education were attending non-Catholic institutions, and he predicted that the number would increase to three-fourths by 1970.[5]

A major problem in Protestant church-related higher education has been the meaning of the relationship between school and church. Although begun under church auspices, many institutions have gradually shifted in character to such an extent that the religious motivation has been virtually submerged. Often these schools are indistinguishable from their public, secular counterparts. Catholicism has experienced no comparable problem. Its schools continue clearly to be creatures of the Church, operated by churchmen and churchwomen. The religious purposes remain central, and students receive an education strongly permeated by the religious ideals of the Church. The availability of such an approved education has caused many members of the Catholic hierarchy to doubt the wisdom of permitting Catholic pupils to attend non-Catholic

---

[5] McCluskey, *op. cit.*, p. 93.

schools. In a recent illustration the head of a Midwestern arch-diocese startled Catholic and non-Catholic alike when he decreed that henceforth all Catholics in his territory would be required to select only Catholic colleges or universities. In his judgment the danger to their faith in other institutions was so great as to make this requirement a necessity. The press gave wide coverage to his announcement, doubtless an indication of the inadequate popular understanding of both canon law and the Catholic philosophy of education.

There is one final pattern of organization in Catholic schools which deserves comment. This is the official policy of sex segregation wherever feasible. Most elementary parochial schools serve both boys and girls, and a few have separate classrooms or divide boys and girls within single classrooms. At the secondary level there is even greater attention to this feature, with individual diocesan schools for boys and girls being maintained. In as much as public education operates on the opposite principle, considerable misunderstanding exists for Catholics and non-Catholics alike. The ideal of separation was stated quite explicitly in the papal encyclical, *The Christian Education of Youth*. It holds that the purposes of education are different for boys and girls. And moral training, particularly in adolescence, needs to be different and explicit. Catholics do not believe that this policy is either unrealistic or that it retards the life adjustments which members of either sex must make to the other. Rather, it is their contention that separate schools create the kind of conditions which permit the Church and families to exercise proper supervision and nurture. Thus, whenever possible, Catholic institutions continue to be separate for the day-to-day educational functions and at the same time sponsor a balanced series of social activities designed to achieve maturation within a pattern that affords full opportunity for adult supervision.

The Teaching of Religion

Since its earliest days, Catholic education has been the peculiar province of the clergy and religious orders. Today there are more than 400 Sisters' groups in America, many with European origins. The Ursuline nuns had arrived in New Orleans by 1727, and during the first decade of the nineteenth century the Visitation sisters opened a school in Georgetown. Mother Elizabeth Seton's parish school in Emmitsburg, Maryland, started in 1810, and the work of the Carmelites in Baltimore culminated in a school by 1831. No less than 138 of the contemporary orders of women are American in origin, having been created to meet the special needs of this nation. Such devotion to education has resulted in more than 75 per cent of today's Catholic school pupils being instructed by sisters.

Similar comments, although proportionately lesser in quantity, could be made about the men. Both ordained clergy and teaching brothers have played a significant role in the vast and rapid cational developments in American Catholicism. The *1964 Official Catholic Directory* reported a total of 191,125 persons engaged in full-time teaching, distributed as follows: priests, 11,697; scholastics, 1126; brothers, 5726; sisters, 104,441; and laymen, 68,135.

Today perhaps the most startling fact about Catholic teachers is the rapid, almost phenomenal, rise in numbers of laymen and laywomen. The population explosion has caused the numbers of Catholic children and youth seeking education at the hands of the Church to far outstrip the increase in quantity of clergy and religious instructors trained and available. As the Church realizes this need, it has been forced to turn increasingly to the lay teacher for staffing its classrooms. For example, between 1946 and 1960 the number of nonreligious instructors engaged in elementary school teaching increased by 900 per cent! If this growth rate continues, and it seems inevitable, by 1971 there will be more lay teachers in the Catholic school system than sisters. This is indeed a revolution when compared to the practices of the past century and a half.

Accompanying this revolution there must be a change in attitude toward the lay Catholic teacher. Too often Catholic parents have assumed that the religious qualities which they sought in their schools inhered in the vocation and person of the clergy or religious order teachers. And the lay teacher has suffered by comparison, being viewed as a poor substitute. Today the Church is faced with raising the money required to attract the most competent laymen into its schools, for it must increasingly delegate to them not only teaching but also administrative tasks. There are no longer sufficient numbers of priests, sisters, and brothers to carry on these functions. And laymen are almost precipitously coming into active, important leadership roles in Catholic education which were denied them only a decade or two ago. Such is the extent of this revolution in teaching staffs which is occurring today.

The teaching of religion is one facet of the Catholic school which is probably more misunderstood by non-Catholics than any

from systematic theological teaching; or, of separating living encounter of God from philosophical and theological interpretation of the experience. And the author concludes her analysis with:

> There must be a scientific approach to the teaching of religion just as for any other subject, and, lest there be any misunderstanding, this means a logical and orderly presentation of the ideas which will stimulate thinking and constructive Christian activity.... Modern catechetics can also, therefore, afford to give more attention than it has so far to incorporating sound educational principles common to all branches of learning.[16]

Similar criticisms on a variety of bases can be found in the literature of Catholic education. Yet, despite their presence, there would appear to be a considerable groundswell of support for this most recent effort to bring to pass more effective religious instruction of the young.

One additional facet of the teaching of religion remains for comment. What of the 50 per cent of Catholic children and youth who have no contact with the schools of the Church? In some parishes there are efforts on the part of the teaching brothers and sisters to instruct these youth after public school attendance. But the majority of this work is done by lay volunteers who are members of the Confraternity of Christian Doctrine. Each diocese has a branch of this organization which guides the instructional activity within the parishes. Nationally established norms call for at least 60 hours in preservice training for these teachers, with additional inservice preparation where possible. And, of course, the Catholic public school pupil often attends a "released-time" class held under the auspices of the Church. More than 4 million were enrolled in these programs during the 1963–64 school year. But, despite all of these efforts, the Catholic student who received all of his nonreligious education outside the Church remains a kind of "second class" member of the parish. The whole range of these supplementary opportunities is insufficient to involve him at comparable depth in the nurturing experiences which the Church provides for its young.

Unresolved Problems for
Future Consideration

The major problem confronting Catholicism's educational work is its inability to reach the almost 50 per cent of children and youth

---

[16] Sister Teresa Mary DeFarrari, "Modern Catechetics—Another View," *The Catholic Educational Review*, LX (November, 1962), 508.

who do not and cannot attend church schools. There have been numerous suggestions offered, and three of them are here considered.

The financing of Catholic schools is done largely from tuition fees, parish, and diocesan funds, and there is general agreement that increased contributions from these sources are virtually impossible. Thus, support for enlargement of the program would have to come chiefly from other places. One warmly debated proposal has been the use of tax funds for private, religious schools. The decade of the 1960's has witnessed an especially spirited exchange of views on this subject.

Proponents of public aid (federal and/or state) argue that Catholics are taxed twice—once for the public schools and again for their parochial institutions. Simple equity should prevail. Further, they observe that the states do require attendance and establish (with compulsory tax funds) public schools to promote the general welfare. But, when a Catholic exercises his freedom of conscience (as guaranteed by *Pierce v. Society of Sisters*), the state denies any comparable support. This is viewed as being, in essence, a religious test used for discriminatory purposes. It is claimed that parochial schools serve the same public service objective that public schools serve. There is really no difference in their contribution to the general welfare. Hence, both types are worthy of public support.

From the legal perspective Catholics see in the Jeffersonian "wall of separation" metaphor an emotional stumbling block to rational discussion. It is often argued by those who oppose public funds for private schools that this separation is absolute. But Catholics observe that this phrase is not a part of the Constitution, and, in fact, there are now and always have been numerous breaches in the "wall." For example, some armed service and congressional chaplains have nothing to do with education. But there has also been both federal and state support for private education for more than 150 years.[17] Thus, it is held that there is no such thing as complete separation. Such matters as federal funds for lunch programs, vocational education, safety and health, and (at least in some states) free textbooks and bus transportation have already established the principle of public support. They conclude that the time has come

---

[17] William W. Brickman and Stanley Lehrer (eds.) *Religion, Government, and Education* (New York: Society for the Advancement of Education, 1961), pp. 111–143.

for sufficient enlargement of this support to enable private, religious schools to accomplish 100 per cent of their task.

But, even while claiming this in principle, most Catholics observe realistically that *direct* support is probably out of the question. While asserting that an inadequate interpretation of the Constitution is involved, Catholics generally admit that such direct subsidies would doubtless be ruled unconstitutional by way of violation of the establishment clause in the First Amendment. Thus, they are forced to turn to and seek *indirect* support. This takes numerous forms. Three typical plans have been selected for illustrative purposes.

One plan proposes a tax credit for sums paid as tuition and fees for education. One recent congressional bill upon which no action was taken provided for a 30 per cent credit for higher education costs. Father Virgil C. Blum has suggested that this practice be applied to elementary and secondary schools as well.[18] In addition to constitutional objections, it is often claimed that any proposal which strengthens private education, whether religious or not, represents a threat to the strength of the public schools.

A second proposal envisages the extension of bus transportation, textbook, and health benefits uniformly to all states. As noted earlier, neither Everson nor Cochran mandated books and buses for Catholic pupils. Their effect was permissive; i.e., where state law permitted, there was no federal objection. Catholics argue that what is acceptable in some states should be extended uniformly to all pupils in all states.

The last form of indirect aid concerns the feasibility of long-term, low-interest loans to parochial schools for capital expenditures. It is argued, with considerable logic, that such loans have already been made available to church-related higher education institutions. Thus, the principle is established. It should now be extended uniformly to education for all age levels.

It is evident therefore that Catholics are striving earnestly to find additional resources for their schools. And various devices have been brought forward to avoid the constitutional issue in seeking public funds. The 1965 Education Act, adopted by the Congress, contains provisions for indirect support to Catholic pupils enrolled in Catholic schools. Although opposed by some Protestant and Jewish groups, the bill had the support of the National Council of

---

[18] Virgil C. Blum, *Freedom of Choice in Education* (New York: The Macmillan Company, 1958).

Churches. But the benefits available to Catholics are minimal, and this small step toward public support will not solve the Catholic financial problem in any significant way. There will doubtless be before each future session of the Congress, as well as some of the state legislatures, new proposals for funds, and each will be accompanied with additional logical and legal justifications for the requests.

Lacking such additional funds for expansion, Catholics have been giving serious consideration to an alternative proposal for a revised pattern of attendance which would involve no new costs. Recognizing that less than one-fourth of Catholics in the 14–18 year age group are in church schools, plus the fact that these are crucial years, a strong minority of Catholic educators has been exploring the feasibility of abandoning the first three or four elementary grades in favor of a concerted emphasis upon the 10–18 year age group. Such a proposal would permit a significant increase in the percentage reached during high school. Many Catholics oppose the idea, usually on the ground that the early years of life are much more determinative than this proposal acknowledges. It is true that many newer parochial schools in recent years have started with the second or third grade, but this principle has not as yet been adopted. It remains a theoretical and untried alternative.

The final proposal for solving the crisis in Catholic education is best represented by a single book which has stirred up much conversation in the past two years. Mary Perkins Ryan, a Catholic who is obviously well-informed about education, wrote *Are Parochial Schools the Answer?*[19] And she answered her question in the negative. Agreeing completely with the goals of the nineteenth century Baltimore councils—the religious education of the young—she questions a continuation of the policy which seems doomed to educate a steadily diminishing proportion of the Catholic population. She proposes renewed attention to the parental role in nurture and the establishment of a supplementary program of catechetical instruction parallel to the general education carried out in public schools. Suggesting that the present system of schools is even weak in religious outcomes with those 50 per cent of pupils reached, Mrs. Ryan proposes a thoroughgoing emphasis upon this supplementary program to reach the total Catholic school-age population.

---

[19] Mary Perkins Ryan, *Are Parochial Schools the Answer?* (New York: Holt, Rinehart & Winston, Inc., 1963).

As might be expected, her book has aroused tremendous criticism. It has generally been rejected for a great variety of reasons. But, despite them all, she has forced renewed attention on the inadequacies of the existing system of education. Her proposals will doubtless not be adopted, but Catholic educators cannot easily be complacent about their shortcomings. Her well-reasoned and pointed criticisms make this impossible any longer.

Catholic education does face a crisis. It is the crisis of its future. And none can be completely certain in what direction this lies in the mid-1960's.

CHAPTER VIII

Other Agencies for Religious
and Moral Education

Interdenominational Organizations

Councils of Churches. The history of cooperative endeavor among denominations in religious education has been outlined in Chapter I. This eventuated in the 1950 establishment of the National Council of the Churches of Christ, U.S.A., and education plays a very prominent part in the total work of this agency.

Local city and county councils of churches are also found today throughout the United States. At the local level a council is the creation of the local churches which have banded together primarily for the purpose of performing cooperatively those functions which they find difficult to do individually. The members at the state level are the denominations rather than local congregations. Almost all local and state councils have departments of education which coordinate leadership development, community programs of weekday religious education, Protestant scouting, campus ministries, youth work, and other similar programs which serve the various churches. In many cities and counties it was the local interdenominational Sunday school association which provided the nucleus around which a council was erected, and such prominence for the role of education has continued to characterize the total programs of today's councils.[1]

At the National level the Division of Christian Education is the agency through which the National Council of Churches accomplishes its educational work. The Division serves as the central coordinating office for the cooperating denominations, aiding them in the development of a comprehensive Christian education service for their constituencies. Through subsidiary departments Christian higher education, as well as missionary education, is included. The

---

[1] John B. Ketcham, "State and Local Councils of Churches and Religious Education," in *Religious Education: A Comprehensive Survey* (ed.) Marvin J. Taylor (Nashville: Abingdon Press, 1960), pp. 327–337.

publishing activity of its predecessor, the International Council of Religious Education, has been continued in the Division. The Revised Standard Version of the Bible is probably its best known product, but the Division, through its commission on curriculum development, also prepares and issues the outlines from which the Uniform Series and Graded Series curriculums are developed by the denominational boards of education and independent publishing houses. It also issues such periodicals as *The International Journal of Religious Education* and *The Christian Scholar*. By means of its Associated Sections the Division encourages and promotes professional association among Christian education workers in annual meetings.[2]

The Cooperative Publication Association is an independent organization whose work is closely related to the National Council. Composed officially of denominational publishers, editors, educators, and representatives of the National Council, the Association exists for the express purpose of publishing those materials which will implement the programs developed in the Division. Committees within the Council prepare recommendations for publications needed, and the Association selects a denominational publisher, obtains an author, and follows the project through to actual publication. Interdenominational leadership texts and other similar materials are among the Association's many publications.

International structures supporting education in the churches date back into the nineteenth century, the first world convention having convened in London in 1889. The World Sunday School Association (WSSA) followed in 1907, and its goals were defined as the holding of conventions, publication of information, and improvement of Sunday schools around the world, but especially in the areas of greatest need. It has discharged these functions faithfully through the years and is known today as the World Council of Christian Education and Sunday School Association (WCCESSA). Offices are maintained in Europe and the United States, with a permanent Far East staff member also. The production of indigenous curriculum materials, the providing of leadership teams, the securing of financial support, and cosponsorship with the World Council of Churches of World Youth Projects are among its major functions. Staff members and short-term leadership teams also provide assistance in the training of national workers around the

---

[2] Gerald E. Knoff, "Christian Education and the National Council of Churches," in *ibid.*, pp. 338–349.

world in the newer nations and their churches. The WCCESSA has been especially active and effective in the decades of the fifties and sixties when so many autonomous nations and churches have appeared. Its official membership is a federation of independent national bodies (denominations and interdenominational agencies), and it performs its services primarily for them. But WCCESSA also serves nonmember churches or countries, upon their request. It thus continues to perform the tasks which were originally established half a century ago.[3]

National Sunday School Association. Conservative Protestantism, whose educational philosophy is considered in Chapter IV, usually, although not always, performs its interdenominational educational work through the National Sunday School Association (NSSA). Organized in 1945, the NSSA is committed to a conservative theological position and is affiliated with the National Association of Evangelicals, whose formation occurred in 1942. A single doctrinal statement is shared by the two associations, and it serves to guide their complementary programs. The NSSA issues its own uniform lesson outlines (which are comparable in structure to those of the National Council of Churches) prepared from the theological perspectives which are contained in its doctrinal statement. It was, in fact, dissatisfaction with the alleged liberal theology of the International Council's uniform series which led to the emergence of the NSSA. Other functions include sponsorship of regional and national Sunday school conventions, publication of literature for religious education, and research and service committee work. Members of the NSSA include some denominations, generally the smaller ones, which have officially joined, local congregations from other denominations which have not affiliated, regional Sunday school associations, and interested individual church members. It publishes an annual *Sunday School Encyclopedia* and a monthly magazine called *Link*. The program is operated through a series of commissions for camp leaders, denominational Sunday school secretaries, directors of education in local churches, publishers, youth and youth leaders, and persons interested in research. The national offices of the National Sunday School Association are located in Chicago.

---

[3] Nelson Chappel, "The World Council of Christian Education and the World Council of Churches," in *ibid.*, pp. 350–358.

Nondenominational Agencies

National Conference of Christians and Jews. Any nation
with a significant degree of religious pluralism faces problems of
intergroup relations. The National Conference of Christians and
Jews (NCCJ) is a product of such strife in the 1920's and particularly in the 1928 presidential election campaign. Founded by
prominent leaders of all three major faiths, NCCJ "exists to promote justice, amity, understanding, and cooperation among Protestants, Catholics, and Jews, and to analyze, moderate, and strive
to eliminate intergroup prejudices. . . ." To this end the Conference engages in an extensive educational program. Its sponsorship
of an annual Brotherhood Week is well known. Through its Religious News Service it seeks to provide understanding and promote
good-will. Its publication program is designed to provide information and teaching materials on human relations. Local offices en-
courage involvement of clergy and laymen in intergroup dialogue
at the community level. It is the goal of NCCJ to provide assistance
toward the pooling of efforts of all leaders (religious, business,
labor, opinion-making, community organizations) in the combat-
ing of prejudice toward religious, racial, nationality, or other
groups. Thus, it finds itself constantly in partnership with church
and synagogue educational leadership in the pursuit of these objectives.[4]

Religious Education Association. At the beginning of the
twentieth century there was widespread dissatisfaction with the
revivalistic nature of the Sunday school and the educational shortcomings of the uniform lessons. The Sunday School Council of
Evangelical Denominations was one of the products of this general
concern. Another was the Religious Education Association. Char-
tered in 1903, the REA was originally Protestant in membership,
but it quickly involved Jews and Catholics in its deliberations and
finally regular membership. Its goals have always been progressive
and pioneering in nature. The original "platform" included a call
for graded curriculum reflecting the best insights known to educators and a comprehensive program which integrated all agencies
(church, school, home) in a united approach to religious education. The response was enthusiastic with thousands of persons af-
filiating in the first few years.

---

4 Dumont F. Kenny, "The National Conference of Christian and Jews," in *ibid.*,
pp. 410–417.

Throughout the decades the organizational structure has gradually changed, but the purpose of REA has remained substantially that of its founders. The membership is genuinely multi-faith, and includes a considerable variety of professions and disciplines. All join as individuals, none formally representing his religious group or institution. The work of the Association is carried out through several means: frequent national conventions on topics of paramount interest; commissions which pursue work in areas of importance to religious education (i.e., higher education, research); a national staff headed by a general secretary; local chapters in major cities; and a bimonthly journal. *Religious Education,* the official periodical, is generally accepted as the most substantial publication in the field of religious education. Its content reflects the pluralistic nature of the Association's membership. The REA continues its exploratory work on the frontiers of the religious movement, seeking always to widen horizons and perspectives in all three faith groups.[5]

Youth-Serving Agencies with Religious Purposes

The United States has an abundance of voluntary associations many of which exist for the welfare of children and youth. Some have no explicit religious purposes, but any agency which promotes good health, intergroup relations, and citizenship is certainly an ally of church and synagogue. Boys' Clubs, Four-H Clubs, and Future Farmers of America are typical of these generally secularly oriented organizations whose work is viewed by religious leaders as worthy but complementary.

In addition there are several agencies whose origins can be found within the framework of organized religion. Camp Fire Girls, Boy and Girl Scouts, YMCA, YWCA, and the YM&WHA are typical of this affiliation. The first three of these agencies operate a significant portion of their programs through local church-sponsored units. The churches provide housing, leadership, financial, and other support for the group. In instances of this church sponsorship the total religious education program of the congregation is simply assumed to include this function. The latter three agencies tend to have building- or camp-centered work although by no means ex-

---

[5] Herman E. Wornom, "The Religious Education Association," *Religious Education,* LVIII (September–October, 1963), 443–452.

clusively. Their religious purpose is explicit, and cooperative relationships are regularly established with nearby churches and synagogues.

At the national level Protestantism seeks to coordinate church and agency work through a National Council of Churches Church-Agency Committee. Denominational and agency representatives comprise its membership. In local communities similar committees have been established in recent years. In each instance the goal is a recognition of the fact that religious and moral education must be integrated rather than compartmentalized or competitive, and the community relationships promote understanding, good-will, and cooperation.[6]

Higher Education and Religion

The Bible College Movement. The Bible Institute-College is a recent phenomenon on the American higher education scene. The earliest founders sought primarily to train laymen to be effective witnesses to their personal faith. Only gradually has the focus shifted to professional preparation for the varying Christian vocations. The first institute opened in Nyack, New York, in 1882, followed by the Moody Bible Institute in Chicago four years later. Others have appeared regularly until more than 250 individual institutions were in existence in 1963.

Initially the program was almost solely biblical and theological in nature. Little attention was given to academic admission standards, and certificates were granted all who completed satisfactorily a stated course of studies. Gradually students sought professional training for all types of ministry, and the question of academic standards has become a continuing concern. Since 1947 an Accrediting Association of Bible Colleges has been the instrument by which these standards were established and utilized. In 1963 only 15 per cent of the schools had met these conditions and been awarded accreditation.

The curriculum of the Bible institute-college differs from that of the liberal arts college primarily at the point of its emphasis on Bible study. At least one full year must be devoted to biblical or related courses specialized for the purpose of Christian vocational training. Liberal arts areas of curriculum are included, but their

---

[6] See *International Journal of Religious Education,* XXXV (September, 1958), a special issue devoted to consideration of church-agency relationships.

role is always subordinate to that of the theological department. Institutions which usually grant no degrees and have a three-year program are called institutes. Some institutions have lengthened their course to four, or even five years, and they award an A.B. degree in Bible. They may actually offer and require a second liberal arts major, but the primary emphasis remains on the Bible and the study of theology. All students in both institute and college are undergraduates, in contrast to those in theological seminaries. There is one other significant distinguishing characteristic of these institutions: they uniformly affirm a quite conservative theological position.[7]

Colleges and Universities. The great majority of higher education institutions established before the Civil War were begun either by churches or for distinctly religious purposes. Hence, the role of religion in both the curriculum and the total educational life of students was significant. Colleges also provided the professional training for church vocations. But much as the nature of elementary and secondary education changed, so did that of higher institutions. As scholarly knowledge expanded, the curriculum was gradually broadened and new departments created. In the universities, a group of colleges (and later graduate schools) were banded together. In the midst of these far-reaching changes, even in colleges which remained church-related, the role of religion was altered and almost always diminished.

Today two major patterns are evident. In tax-supported institutions attention to religion varies from none up to considerable. Judaism and the major Christian groups have a wide range of religious foundations adjacent to campuses for worship, fellowship, and informal instruction. Departments of religion and courses in religion in other departments are not unusual. At least one school of religion exists as a part of a large, mid-western state university. Chaplains and chapels are also found in several of the states. The legal question, i.e., the significance of "separation of church and state," remains clouded. But there does appear to be an increasing interest in religion on these campuses particularly in the elective university curriculum.

There are also several hundred private, church-related colleges and universities for whom there is no legal problem. Many have

---

[7] S. A. Witmer, "The Bible Institute and Bible College Movement," in *An Introduction to Evangelical Christian Education* (ed.) J. Edward Hakes (Chicago: Moody Press, 1964), pp. 379–391.

been content to define church-relatedness in terms of a department of religion, the availability of a chaplain, and other compartmentalized phenomena. Other aspects of the program have not been too dissimilar from comparable functions performed in secular institutions. But since World War II a remarkable shift of focus has been occurring. There has been a forthright search for "Christian distinctiveness," and faculties and administrations have sought to redefine educational objectives in such a manner as to give religious perspectives an integrative and central role. Departments of religion, chaplains, chapels, required courses, and other traditional features have continued and been strengthened. But the definition of the Christian college is seldom confined to such functions today. Religious faith is seen as an important distinguishing characteristic of the total institution. As a result church-relatedness has taken on new and deeper meaning in many institutions.[8]

In Conclusion

One might well summarize religious and moral education, as they are found in our schools and churches, by pointing out the unrest and change which are evident. Old established patterns which formerly were thought to be adequate for meeting needs are under attack, and nothing seems firmly established. Not even the parochial school within Roman Catholicism has escaped this challenge, and there are those proponents of more effective religious nurture who seriously propose its abandonment for an alternative approach. And many who would still defend the school's validity are willing to consider a radical change in its focus, moving primarily from major attention to elementary education toward the secondary school years. Similar, though more diverse, tendencies are obvious within Protestantism. Except for those few denominations who have adopted day schools, few if any Protestants through the decades have criticized the near exclusive reliance upon the church school. It has stood as the unquestioned medium for the achievement of all educational objectives. But this day is also now past. Competent, responsible educational commentators are proposing new approaches to educational strategy, ideas which could replace

---

[8] See, for example, supplements to *The Christian Scholar,* XXXVII (Autumn, 1954), and XLI (Autumn, 1958) for reports of national conferences on the nature of Christian higher education. See also, *The Mission of the Christian College in the Modern World,* Addresses and Reports of the 3rd Quadrennial Convocation of Christian Colleges (Washington, D.C.: Council of Protestant Colleges and Universities, 1962).

the lay, volunteer programs which now predominate. And this same concern for effectiveness is everywhere manifest in the Jewish community. While still statistically rather insignificant, the phenomenal growth of the Jewish day-school movement symbolizes the uneasiness of Jewish parents. But those who rely solely upon after public school supplementary patterns are equally apprehensive, as their varied suggestions for strengthening their offerings all indicate. All in all, organized religious education has moved away from complacency and self-satisfaction to a clear recognition of its educational inadequacies and some tentative efforts at improvement.

There is also potentially a new day dawning within the public school. We have witnessed a trend of more than a century of elimination of religious influences and content. In perspective, the reason for this now seems clear. The religious practices abandoned were most often sectarian and devotional in nature. But today the school has a new opportunity afforded by the 1963 Court decision. The study about religion, an educational rather than devotional exercise, has received clear approval. Hence, religious literacy can now become at least an elective province of the public school, and concerned religionists have a legal right to ask their schools to assume this responsibility. This, plus the established patterns of moral and spiritual value emphases, seems to give the public school an opportunity to re-establish a concern for religious development, or at least that phase of it which is intellectual and clearly educational.

Bibliography

Bower, William C., and Percy R. Hayward, *Protestantism Faces Its Educational Task Together*. Appleton, Wisconsin: C. C. Nelson Publishing Co., 1949.

Butler, J. Donald, *Religious Education: The Foundations and Practice of Nurture*. New York: Harper & Row, Publishers, 1962.

Butts, R. Freeman, *The American Tradition in Religion and Education*. Boston: Beacon Press, Inc., 1950.

Dierenfield, Richard B., *Religion in American Public Schools*. Washington, D.C.: Public Affairs Press, 1962.

Dushkin, Alexander M., and Uriah Z. Engelman, *Jewish Education in the United States*. New York: The American Association for Jewish Education, 1959.

Educational Policies Commission, *Moral and Spiritual Values in the Public Schools*. Washington, D.C.: National Education Association, 1951.

Fallaw, Wesner, *Church Education for Tomorrow*. Philadelphia: The Westminster Press, 1960.

Hakes, J. Edward, ed., *An Introduction to Evangelical Christian Education*. Chicago: Moody Press, 1964.

Little, Sara, *The Role of the Bible in Contemporary Christian Education*. Richmond, Virginia: John Knox Press, 1961.

Lynn, Robert W., *Protestant Strategies in Education*. New York: Association Press, 1964.

McCluskey, Neil G., *Catholic Viewpoint on Education* (rev. ed.). Garden City, N.Y.: Doubleday & Company, Inc., 1962.

Miller, Randolph Crump, *Education for Christian Living* (2nd ed.). Englewood Cliffs, N.J.: Prentice-Hall, Inc., 1963.

Sloyan, Gerard S., ed., *Modern Catechetics: Message and Method in Religious Formation*. New York: The Macmillan Company, 1963.

Taylor, Marvin J., ed., *Religious Education: A Comprehensive Survey*. Nashville: Abingdon Press, 1960.

Wyckoff, D. Campbell, *Theory and Design of Christian Education Curriculum*. Philadelphia: The Westminster Press, 1961.

Index